MEN AND WOMEN

EQUAL YET DIFFERENT

A Brief Study of the
Biblical Passages on Gender

Alexander Strauch

Lewis & Roth Publishers
P.O. Box 469 • Littleton, CO • 80160
United States of America

About the Author:
Alexander Strauch has served in the leadership and teaching ministry of Littleton Bible Chapel (near Denver, Colorado) for nearly 50 years. As a gifted Bible teacher and a church elder with extensive practical experience, Mr. Strauch has taught in more than 25 countries and has helped thousands of churches worldwide through his expository writing ministry. Other works by Mr. Strauch include: *Biblical Eldership*, *Paul's Vision for the Deacons*, *Agape Leadership*, *The Hospitality Commands*, *Meetings That Work*, *Love or Die*, *Leading With Love*, *If You Bite & Devour One Another* and *The 15 Descriptions of Love*.

Cover Design: Eric Anderson (resolutiondesign.com)
Editor: Amanda Sorenson

College Press Publishing Company has generously given permission to use numerous quotations from *Gender Roles & the Bible: Creation, the Fall, & Redemption,* by Jack Cottrell. Copyright 1994.

Scripture taken from the NEW AMERICAN STANDARD BIBLE, Copyright 1960, 1962, 1963, 1968, 1972, 1973, 1975, 1977, 1995 by The Lockman Foundation. Used by permission.

Library of Congress Cataloging-in-Publication Data

Strauch, Alexander, 1944-
     Men and women, equal yet different: a brief study of the biblical
passages on gender / Alexander Strauch.
          p.   cm.
     Includes bibliographical references and indexes.
     ISBN 0-936083-16-6
          1. Sex role—Religious aspects—Christianity—History of
doctrines—Early church, ca. 30-600. 2. Women—Biblical teaching.
3. Bible. N.T.-Criticism, interpretation, etc.   I. Title.
II. Title: Equal yet different.
BT708.S84   1999
261.8'343—dc21   99-32861

                                                                    CIP

ISBN: 0-93608-316-6
Printed in the United States of America
Thirteenth Printing / 2019
www.lewisandroth.com

To receive a free catalog of books published by Lewis & Roth Publishers, call toll free: 800-477-3239 (USA and Canada). For local and international customers, call 719-494-1800.

STATEMENT OF PURPOSE

One of the most significant changes in human history has occurred during the past forty years. It is the gender revolution. In the words of historian William Manchester, "the erasure of distinctions between the sexes is not only the most striking issue of our time, it may be the most profound the race has ever confronted."[1]

Like the rest of society, Christianity has been permanently affected by this change. According to a leading *Time* magazine article entitled "The Second Reformation," religious feminists "believe they are caught up in one of Christendom's great and historic transformations."[2] In reality, the gender transformation taking place within the worldwide Christian community is not a sign of a "second reformation" (the first being Martin Luther's back-to-the Bible, sixteenth-century reformation) but of a radical departure from biblical, apostolic Christianity.

Among Bible-believing Christians, the gender revolution has spawned intense, emotional controversy over what the Bible says about the roles of men and women. There are two major viewpoints in this debate. One is the evangelical feminist view (or egalitarian view); the other is the complementarian view, which is the non-feminist view.

The purpose of this book is to state and defend the complementarian viewpoint. Written in outline form, the book presents biblical evidence that Jesus Christ taught that men and women are equal yet different. It introduces the key terms, arguments, and most recent research related to the complementarian position. Thus it also provides an easy-to-read summary of all the key Scripture passages commonly used in the gender debate.

Ninety percent of this book consists of Scripture exposition. I emphasize the Scriptures because the answer to this debate is found in God's Word, not in books on sociology or anthropology. Furthermore, "no factor is more influential in shaping a [Christian's] moral and social behavior than regular Bible reading."[3] Yet biblical illiteracy abounds in alarming proportions among Christians today,[4] and one well-known authority predicts an even greater decline in Bible reading.[5] As the voices of postmodern secular society grow louder and more appealing, it is essential that Christians hear clearly the voice of God through the Word of God in order to counteract secular society's pervasive influence.

I sincerely pray that you will find the careful exposition of Holy Scripture to be the most rewarding part of this book. The study of God's Word should always be exciting for a Christian. Our Lord loved the Word of God and quoted it with full authority when He faced trials and controversy. As one biblical scholar aptly says of Jesus, our Lord,

> We can say with all reverence that Jesus Christ was practically saturated with the Scriptures.... One tenth of His words were taken from the Old Testament. In the Four Gospels 180 of 1,800 verses which report His discourses are either quotations of the written revelation or else direct allusions to it. If we are criticized for constantly quoting Scripture texts, what can be said of Christ, who had them constantly at the tip of His tongue?[6]

This book is written for people who are unfamiliar with the biblical passages on gender and probably will not read a lengthy technical book on the subject (of which there are a bewildering number of choices). It is especially suitable for high school- and college-age young people. It is also an excellent resource for anyone who wants an overview of all the key biblical passages related to the gender debate from the complementarian position.

If we are criticized for constantly quoting Scripture texts, what can be said of Christ, who had them constantly at the tip of His tongue? RENÉ PACHE

As to the spiritual identity of my readers, I take for granted that they accept the lordship of Jesus Christ over their lives and believe the Bible to be the written Word of God and the Christian's divine, unerring authority for doctrine and life. As the Bible says of itself,

> All Scripture is inspired by God [literally, God-breathed] and profitable for teaching, for reproof, for correction, for training in righteousness; so that the man of God may be adequate, equipped for every good work (2 Tim. 3:16, 17).

Understanding the Controversy

Tom, a freshman at a well-known Christian college, stops me after church one Sunday and says, "I'm really confused about the roles of men and women in the church."

"Why?" I ask.

"Some of my professors say that God made men and women as equals and that traditional gender roles are a myth, a simplistic interpretation of the Bible. Other professors insist that the Bible teaches both equality and gender role differences."

"Well," I laugh, "you've been introduced to the gender debate. I got thoroughly involved in it during the early '70s. Over the years, it has been a personal interest to follow this debate, especially its impact among Bible-believing churches. In fact, the heat keeps rising and the books and articles keep rolling off the presses. It's a hot one!"

"What should I do?" he asks.

"How concerned are you?" I inquire.

"A lot," he insists.

"Why?"

"Because I want to know what God wants me to do. I want to know what the Bible says."

"Good, Tom! I'm glad to hear that you want to know what the Bible, God's Word, teaches. Let's get together and study it. I'll show you why I have come to believe that the Bible teaches that God made men and women as equal yet different."

The gender debate is not an abstract, impersonal, doctrinal controversy. It touches directly on our humanness, our sexual identity, our ministry opportunities, the marriage relationship, family life, and life in the local church. It raises fundamental issues regarding fairness and justice, the influence of secular culture on Christian thinking, the correct methods for interpreting

God's Word, the leadership of our churches, and our faith in God's Word. It is an emotionally charged controversy that divides churches and denominations worldwide.

As my young friend discovered, no one can hide from this issue. Nor should one try to avoid it. It's too important. The gender debate challenges our thinking and our fundamental beliefs, which is good. Such controversial issues drive serious-minded believers to think more accurately and to study God's Word more diligently.

When I was 18 years old, for example, two Jehovah's Witnesses shook my faith down to bedrock. They challenged my beliefs regarding the deity of Christ. They threw questions at me that I couldn't answer, nor could anyone else I knew. Through prayer, by reading all I could on the subject, and by diligent, conscientious study of Scripture, I finally could answer their questions from the Bible. Their challenge resulted in the strengthening of my faith and the development of my ability to search the Scriptures.

Although the gender debate is not on the same level of doctrinal centrality as is a challenge to the deity of Christ, it is nevertheless a significant issue. It, too, forces us to examine our closely held beliefs and discover what the Bible actually says.

Bible-believing Christians generally hold one of two positions regarding the gender debate. One position is the complementarian view (pronounced, Com ple men TAIR ee un), which is the non-feminist view. It is also called the traditional or hierarchical view. The other position is the evangelical feminist view or egalitarian view (pronounced, EE gal iTAIR ee un). It is also known as biblical feminism, biblical egalitarianism, or biblical equality. Most people who hold the complementarian viewpoint would rather refer to their viewpoint as the biblical one. But since adherents of both sides of the debate claim to hold the biblical view, I will employ the terms *complementarian* and *evangelical feminist* in order to distinguish the two major interpretations.

Complementarian View

The complementarian view teaches that God created men and women as equals with different gender-defined roles. Scholars chose the term *complementarian* in order to emphasize both the equality of the sexes and the complementary differences between men and women. According to this viewpoint, God created men and women equally in His divine image. Men and women are fully equal in personhood, dignity, and worth (Genesis 1:26-28). Furthermore, complementarians assert, all believers in Jesus Christ—whether male or female—are baptized, Spirit-gifted, believer-priests and are full members of the Body of Christ. Therefore, they should use their spiritual gifts to their fullest potential and grow in their faith to full spiritual maturity.

According to the complementarian viewpoint, it is equally true that God created men and women to be different and to fulfill distinct gender roles. God designed the man to be husband, father, provider, protector. He is to be head of the family and to lead the church family. God designed the woman to be wife, mother, nurturer. She is to actively help and submit to the man's leadership. God designed these differences at creation. The Bible uses key terms like *head, helper,* and *submission* to describe these differences, which are our sovereign Creator's wise design for His image-bearing creation.

To correctly represent the biblical teaching on gender, both truths—equality and role differences—need to be affirmed and held in balanced tension. When properly understood and practiced, these role differences promote godly manhood and womanhood and marvelously enrich family life as well as life in the local church. God is profoundly concerned that gender differences not be minimized or blurred. These differences are fundamental to our sexual identity as male and female and thus need to be better understood and developed according to Scripture.

Adherents of the complementarian view believe that it best represents the plain, literal, straightforward teaching of the Bible on gender. Furthermore, role differences are clearly and repeatedly taught and practiced by Jesus Christ and His apostles. This view also represents the historic interpretation followed by churches and Christian teachers over the past two thousand years, although at times it has been imperfectly understood and implemented.

To correctly represent the biblical teaching on gender, both truths—equality and role differences—need to be affirmed and held in balanced tension.

Despite God's design for harmonious male-female relationships, the fall of mankind into sin, recorded in Genesis 3, created the battle of the sexes. Sinful men and women have corrupted God's plan for male-female relationships, and the consequences, particularly to women, have been detrimental. Even so, as believers in Jesus Christ, Christian men and women can rediscover, understand, and practice God's design for the sexes.

> **A Major Organization Representing the Complementarian View**
> The complementarian position is represented by an organization called Council for Biblical Manhood and Womanhood (CBMW), founded in 1987. Its position paper is the *Danvers Statement*. CBMW also publishes the *Journal for Biblical Manhood and Womanhood*. You can obtain more information about this organization and its publications by writing to CBMW, 2825 Lexington Rd., Box 926, Louisville, KY 40280. Web site: **www.cbmw.org**

Evangelical Feminist View

Evangelical feminists teach that God created men and women equally to bear the divine image. Furthermore, they conclude that true equality requires equal ministry opportunities for both sexes. They believe that the submission of the woman in marriage and womanly restrictions in Christian ministry are inconsistent with the true picture of biblical equality. They consider the equal-yet-different doctrine taught by complementarians to be a contradiction in terms.

According to the evangelical feminist view, true biblical equality assures that both men and women are full and equal partners in life. The concept of mutual submission and responsibility determines the relationship between men and women in both marriage and the church. Women and men are free to exercise in the church any and all gifts they possess. Men hold no unique, leadership-authority role solely because of their gender. Leadership and teaching in the church is to be determined by spiritual gift and ability, not gender.

This viewpoint recognizes that men and women are not identical. Sexual and other differences between men and women are to be enjoyed, but not exaggerated out of proportion. One's gender does not determine one's status or role in life, nor does it limit spiritual giftedness and ministry opportunities. A woman who is gifted by God to teach and lead the church deserves to have equal opportunity to exercise her giftedness.

Adherents of this viewpoint consider the Bible's statements on headship

---

According to evangelical feminists, one's gender does not determine one's status or role in life, nor does it limit spiritual giftedness and ministry opportunities.

---

and submission to have been grossly misinterpreted by past generations of Christians. They believe that simplistic, literal, and traditional interpretations of the Scriptures misrepresent the Bible's teaching on gender equality. As a result, women have been discriminated against and their gifts and services have been wasted. Furthermore, they believe that male domination of women is the result of sin entering the world, as recorded in Genesis 3. In their view, Christ's work on the cross restores the original equality of the sexes that is envisioned in Genesis 2 because in Christ "there is neither male nor female" (Gal. 3:28).

A Major Organization Representing the Evangelical Feminist View
The evangelical feminist position is represented best by an organization called Christians for Biblical Equality (CBE). Its position paper is *Men, Women & Biblical Equality.* You can obtain more information about this organization by writing to CBE, 122 West Franklin Avenue, Suite 218, Minneapolis, MN, 55404. Web site: **www.cbeinternational.org**

Jesus Christ and Gender Discrimination

No one who truly loves people, is sensitive to the Word of God, and is keenly aware of the unspeakable dehumanization that women have suffered (and still suffer) would want to discriminate against women (see summary entitled "War Against Women" at the end of this chapter). To sin against women is to sin against God in whose image women are created.

Why, then, would any intelligent, thinking, sensitive, Bible-believing Christian dare argue for role distinctions between men and women? The answer is simple: Jesus Christ taught that men and women are equal yet different. Although He taught and practiced gender-based role distinctions, Jesus Christ treated all women, even those who were considered to be outcasts of society, with dignity (Luke 7:36-50). He communicated the gospel message to women with love and compassion. In turn, women followed Him and loved Him. They felt free to approach Him.

As Bible-believing Christians, we would never think of accusing Jesus Christ of sin against women or male chauvinism. He alone is absolutely perfect; we are imperfect. He is God in flesh, Truth incarnate. He is the supreme reference point, the final Word. Upon the cross, Jesus suffered for the sins committed by men against women, as well as women's sins against men. He bore these sins in His body on the cross. Thus the gospel provides forgiveness and healing for the cruel injustices men and women have committed against one another.

Yet Jesus Christ practiced role distinctions between the sexes by designating male leadership for His Church. In our zeal to right the horrible wrongs that have been committed against women, we must be careful not to violate the truth of God's Word and God's design for the sexes. We must not forget that God created male-female role distinctions in order for the sexes to beautifully complement each other and to exercise different functions in society. His intention for distinct gender roles is good and fair.

Despite God's good intent for gender distinctions, sin has corrupted such distinctions and made them a cause for discrimination and abuse. Secular society's only solution to gender discrimination is to declare complete gender equality. For many in our society, gender equality is an unquestioned assumption—like gravity. Any alternative to equality is incomprehensible to the modern mind. But the teaching of Jesus Christ provides an alternative: God created men and women with equal dignity yet designed them to fulfill different roles. To a Bible-believing Christian, what Jesus Christ says determines what is right and wrong. He defines what is discrimination and what is proper order between the sexes. Secular society does not define these for us.

Jesus Christ has the solution to our gender-confused world. The evils perpetuated against women did not arise from Jesus' teaching or practice. They are the result of sin in the human heart and are part of the larger picture of mankind's sinful inhumanity to mankind. To paraphrase Jesus, evil thoughts, murders, adulteries, and gender abuse proceed out of the heart (Mark 7:23).

In our zeal to right the horrible wrongs that have been committed against women, we must be careful not to violate the truth of God's Word and God's design for the sexes.

A Plea

I want those who are undecided about the Bible's teaching on gender to know that complementarians deeply desire that all women be treated justly and with dignity. We abhor male chauvinistic superiority and the abuse of women. We are aware that some Christian theologians, husbands, and churches have misused the Bible to say degrading things about and to commit crimes against women, for which we are ashamed. But as you will discover through this book, *Christlike love* adds a divine and mutually beneficial character to the role differences between Christian men and women.

I hope you will come to understand that although sinful men and women have misunderstood and abused the doctrine of headship and submission, the doctrine itself is rooted in God's wisdom and love. When it is applied in love, it reflects God's design for the sexes. We complementarians do not hold this viewpoint because we want to maintain archaic, legalistic traditions or male supremacy. Rather, we uphold it because we believe that Jesus Christ taught both gender equality and gender-based role distinctions.

What Jesus Christ says determines what is right and wrong. He defines what is discrimination and what is proper order between the sexes. Secular society does not define these for us.

Human traditions can blind the minds of even the best people. Jesus Christ Himself was put to death by religious people who placed man-made, legalistic traditions above God's Word. For complementarians, gender is an issue of "thus says the Lord." We believe in role distinctions because the Bible teaches them, and the Bible is the Word of God.

War Against Women

Although in certain countries women have made enormous advancements, "much of the world is still waging war against women."[7] The World Conference on Human Rights (1993) declares that there is a worldwide epidemic of violence against women.[8] When speaking to the General Assembly of the United Nations, Secretary General Kofi Annan said, "Violence against women has become the most pervasive human rights violation, respecting no distinction of geography, culture or wealth."[9]

According to the 1993 United Nation's Human Development Report, "no country treats its women as well as it treats its men."[10] Women throughout the world suffer a greater degree of poverty than men. Two thirds of the world's illiterates are women.[11] In many parts of the world, women are denied basic human rights. They are forced into low-skilled jobs, are underpaid, are overworked, and are discriminated against. Even in modern, developed societies, divorce leaves women with the primary responsibility to care for the children and usually leaves them in a greater degree of poverty than their estranged husbands.

Sexual assault on young girls, rape, and wife beating are rampant worldwide and remain seriously underreported.[12] In the Philippines, Thailand, and India, the forced prostitution of young girls continues on almost unchecked; there is a growing transnational girl-child slave industry. In India (especially northern India) bride burning continues, and more than nine thousand brides a year are killed by husbands or in-laws who seek a second dowry.[13] In parts of Africa, young girls undergo forced genital mutilation (female circumcision), in part to curb future sexual desire. Furthermore, the worldwide explosion of hard-core pornography degrades all women because it vividly imprints on men's minds that a woman's value is primarily for sex.

In Afghanistan, the repression of women defies belief. Women are denied basic, humane medical care and education. They cannot even go out in public without a male family member and must be completely covered from head to foot. Islamic militants threaten death to any women who speak out against injustice. The situation is so extreme that it has been called "gender apartheid."

The ultimate violence and contempt for women, however, is the practice of female infanticide and sex-selection abortion. Modern technology provides parents in Third World countries such as China and India the ability to detect the sex of a fetus in order to dispose of unwanted baby girls. By choice, males are more numerous in these countries, creating a serious deficiency of wives for men. It is estimated that in South and East Asia, because of infanticide, high maternal mortality, and nutritional and health neglect, "some 100 million women are 'missing.'"[14] Such statistics should cause us to weep. In the words of *Time* magazine, "there are precious few female-friendly spots on earth."[15]

Whether we are egalitarians or complementarians, we can agree that we need to speak out against and work to eliminate such terrible injustices to women.

Questions for "Statement of Purpose"

1. What are your main questions or concerns regarding the gender debate?
2. Identify the major theme of this book, which the author seeks to prove from Scripture.
3. What do each of the following Scripture texts teach about Jesus Christ's attitude toward and belief in Holy Scripture?
   Matthew 4:1-11, 5:18,15:3, 4, 6
   Luke 18:31, 24:25-27, 32, 44
   John 10:34, 35
4. What attitude does Acts 17:11 suggest a believer should have toward debatable issues and the use of Scripture?
5. What evidence do you see that "biblical illiteracy abounds in alarming proportions among Christians today"?
6. If biblical illiteracy continues to increase, what may be the consequences to our churches?

Questions for "Understanding the Controversy"

1. Why is it vitally important for a Bible-believing Christian to thoroughly understand the controversy related to gender roles? In what ways does this debate affect you personally?
2. Where do you go first to find answers to questions concerning gender? Why?
3. What does male chauvinism mean? Use a dictionary to help you answer this question.
4. What does the word egalitarian mean? Use a dictionary to help you answer this question.
5. In one or two sentences summarize the complementarian position.
6. In one or two sentences summarize the evangelical feminist position.
7. Why has evangelical feminism become so popular today among Bible believing Christians? What is its appeal?
8. Do complementarians sinfully discriminate against women because they believe in role differences between men and women? If not, why not?
9. In what ways did the information in the box entitled, "War Against Women," influence your thinking on gender issues?
10. What new information did you learn from these two sections? How does this information help shape your thinking and actions?

OUTLINE

I. JESUS CHRIST APPEALED TO THE CREATION ACCOUNT

L et's start studying," Tom says.
"I would love to!" I respond.

"Where do we begin?" he asks.

"We begin where Jesus began."

"Jesus Christ?"

"Yes, Jesus said in John 13:13, 'You call Me Teacher and Lord; and you are right, for so I am.' We turn to Jesus Christ because He is our Lord and Teacher. He directs our course of study. He shows us where to begin."

"And just where is that?"

"In the Old Testament. Jesus points us back to the original creation accounts in Genesis 1 and 2, so that is where we start our study."

"How do we know that Jesus begins there?" Tom asks.

"When Jesus was questioned by a delegation of Pharisees about the long-debated issue of divorce, He directed His critics to Genesis 1 and 2. In fact, He quoted Genesis 1:27 and 2:24 as the authoritative source of truth. So let's read the account in Matthew 19:3-5."

19:3 Some Pharisees came to Jesus, testing Him and asking, "Is it lawful for a man to divorce his wife for any reason at all?"

19:4 And He answered and said, "Have you not read that He who created them from the beginning made them male and female,

19:5 and said, 'For this reason a man shall leave his father and mother and be joined to his wife, and the two shall become one flesh'?

When responding to the Pharisees' male-centered divorce practice, Jesus declared, "from the beginning it was not so" (Matt. 19:8 NKJV). The Pharisees had failed to understand God's original intention for marriage and the sexes. Hence Jesus told them to go back to the "beginning," back to the Genesis account of creation, back to the Word of God where they would discover

God's normative design for marriage.

The same is true for us today. If we want to understand God's will for the sexes, we must follow Christ's example. When Jesus and His chief representatives, Peter and Paul, wanted to recapture the original design for marriage

---

Jesus Christ, Peter, and Paul affirmed the truthfulness of the Genesis record and based their gender teachings on it.

---

and gender, they used Genesis, the book of "beginnings." Stephen B. Clark, in his colossal work entitled, *Man and Woman in Christ,* echoes this vitally significant point:

> Other New Testament writers, especially Paul, followed Jesus' lead. Most of the important passages on men-women roles in the New Testament refer back either explicitly or implicitly to the first three chapters of Genesis.... It is not possible to understand the New Testament teaching on men and women without understanding how it is founded on the creation of Adam and Eve and on God's purpose as revealed in the creation of the human race.[16]

Since Jesus Christ, Peter, and Paul affirmed the truthfulness of the Genesis record and based their gender teachings on it, we will briefly explore three, essential, bedrock passages: Genesis 1:26-28; Genesis 2:7-25; Genesis 3:1-19.

A. Genesis 1: Created Equal in God's Image

In the ancient world, the Genesis account of the creation of man and woman stands out as truly unique. It is not colored by the pagan, polytheistic religions of the ancient Near East. According to the Genesis narrative, there is only one God who created all things by His Word. He created man and woman uniquely and specifically to bear His image and to represent Him on earth. Moses' declaration of the equality between the sexes was radical for its day: woman, as well as man, bore the stamp of God's divine image. The first man enthusiastically prized and loved the first woman. She was not his property nor was she his slave.

As familiar as they may be, do not rush over these incredibly profound and theologically significant passages of Scripture. Carefully read the following verses from Genesis 1:

> **1:26** Then God said, "Let Us make man [Hebrew: *'adam,* meaning *man* in the sense of "mankind," "human race"] in Our image, according to Our likeness; and let them rule over...all the earth."
>
> **1:27** God created man in His own image, in the image of God He created him; male and female He created them.
>
> **1:28** God blessed them; and God said to them, "Be fruitful and multiply, and fill the earth, and subdue it; and rule over... every living thing that moves on the earth."

Note the following observations:

1. God created the human race male and female.

God created two sexually distinct human beings, the male human and the female human. He designed sexuality and called it good. God didn't have to create separate male and female humans. He could have created female humans with the capacity to reproduce themselves. He didn't have to make male humans. But God had specific purposes in mind when He created two sexually distinct human beings. One purpose is to teach His people spiritual truths concerning His relationship with them, especially through the one-flesh union of two distinct persons in marriage (see Eph. 5:29-32).

**The fact that both sexes individually bear God's
image demonstrates that they are equal
in dignity and being.**

---

2. God created both the man and the woman in His image.

God stamped His divine image and likeness on both the individual man and the individual woman. Both sexes are image bearers of the one, true God. Nobility, dignity, and eternity mark their faces. They are not like the animals over which they rule.

The fact that both sexes individually bear God's image demonstrates that they are equal in dignity and being. Both are equally necessary and important to God's design for the human race.

3. God commanded both the man and the woman to multiply and rule the earth.

God crowned the man and woman as king and queen of the earth. He commanded them to multiply and rule the earth. These mandates are based on the facts that both bear equally the divine image; thus they can rule the earth and give birth to others who bear the same divine image. People say, "It's a man's world," but God says it's His world. He created both men and women as necessary parts of His plan for humans to rule and fill the earth.

4. God named the human race "man."

Verse 26 states, "Let Us make man in Our image." The word "man" is used here in the sense of "mankind," or "human race," not in the sense of male gender. This use of the word *man* is called the generic use.[17] It includes men and women as a class, that is, as human beings.

What is noteworthy is that God chose to use the name of one of the sexes, *man,* to designate the whole race. In Genesis 5:1, 2 this is even more clearly brought out: "This is the book of the generations of Adam [Hebrew: *'adam*]. In the day when God created man [*'adam*], He made him in the likeness of God. He created them male and female, and He blessed them and *named them Man* [*'adam*] in the day when they were created" (italics added). God didn't use the term *woman* genetically to describe the whole human race. He didn't say, "Let us make woman in Our image." Nor did He say, "Let us make mortals in Our image." He said, "man."

Raymond Ortlund, Jr., one of the contributors to the classic volume *Recovering Biblical Manhood and Womanhood,* observes that "God's naming of the race 'man' whispers male headship, which Moses will bring forward boldly in chapter two [of Genesis]."[18]

B. Genesis 2: Created Equal and Different

We now come to Genesis chapter 2, a crucial, decisive passage for our study. It is a battleground chapter. *One cannot understand the gender debate among Bible-believing Christians without grasping its significance.* It is the foundation of the rest of the Bible's teaching on gender. This is the chapter that is foremost in the minds of Christ and His apostles when they teach on marriage and gender roles. Old Testament commentator Derek Kidner expresses well the critically significant nature of verses 18-25: "The New Testament draws much of its teaching on the sexes from this crowning paragraph of the chapter, which is the dynamic, or dramatic, counterpart of 1:27, 28."[19]

Genesis 2 is the chapter that is foremost in the minds of Christ and His apostles when they teach on marriage and gender roles.

Genesis 2 prepares you for the New Testament material that lies ahead. So read this chapter, meditate on it, and master it. Take special note of the verses below.

2:7 Then the LORD God formed man [*ha 'adam,* the male human being, Adam] of dust from the ground, and breathed into his nostrils the breath of life; and man became a living being.

2:15 Then the LORD God took the man and put him into the garden of Eden to cultivate it and keep it.

2:16 The LORD God commanded the man, saying, "From any tree of the garden you may eat freely;

2:18 Then the LORD God said, "It is not good for the man to be alone; I will make him a helper suitable for him."

2:19 Out of the ground the LORD God formed every beast of the field and every bird of the sky, and brought them to the man to see what he would call them; and whatever the man called a living creature, that was its name.

2:21 So the LORD God caused a deep sleep to fall upon the man, and he slept; then He took one of his ribs, and closed up the flesh at that place.

2:22 The LORD God fashioned into a woman the rib which He had taken from the man, and brought her to the man.

2:23 The man said, "This is now bone of my bones, And flesh of my flesh; She shall be called Woman, Because she was taken out of Man."

2:24 For this reason a man shall leave his father and his mother, and be joined to his wife; and they shall become one flesh.

Taken at face value, these verses are scandalous to the ears of most modern secular and religious people. Liberal feminists (religious as well as secular) dismiss Genesis 2 as an ancient myth. They believe it is hopelessly patriarchal and completely irrelevant to twenty-first-century women.

Bible-believing feminists (egalitarians) believe Genesis 2 to be the divinely inspired Word of God. They say, however, that the passage teaches the equality of the sexes only and emphatically deny that Genesis 2 is the foundation passage to the respective headship and subordination roles of men and women.

Egalitarian View of Genesis 2

Mary Stewart Van Leeuwen, professor of psychology at Eastern College and a leading evangelical feminist scholar, makes this bold assertion, "Nor is there any indication in the creation accounts that the man was to take the lead in this process [dominion of the earth]."[20]

Rebecca Groothuis, an articulate spokesperson for evangelical feminism, adds: "The Genesis creation account *cannot justifiably be used to demonstrate* the existence of male authority and female subordination before the fall. Gender hierarchy *cannot be extracted from the Genesis text* unless it is first smuggled into the text" (italics added).[21]

Gilbert Bilezikian, a former professor of biblical studies and a founding elder at Willow Creek Community Church, writes, "Any teaching that inserts an authority structure between Adam and Eve in God's creation design [Genesis 1 -2] is to be firmly rejected since it is not founded on the biblical text."[22]

Genesis 2, however, presents the six vital truths that are essential to our understanding of the New Testament teaching on gender. These truths, outlined below, prepare us for further study.

1. God made Adam the central character.

Jack Cottrell, professor of theology at Cincinnati Bible Seminary, correctly states, "All the action and events revolve around the man.... he occupies center stage. Everything else, including the woman, has a supporting role."[23] Cottrell goes on to demonstrate this critical point:

> The male, not the female, is given the name—the generic name—borne by the human race as a whole: Adam, or Man (2:5; see 1:26 and 5:2). The male is the one to whom God speaks in the narrative (2:16); he is the first to receive divine revelation and instruction. The animals are brought for naming to the male, not the female (2:19,20). The woman is made from

the man, not the man from the woman (2:22). The woman is also made for the man and brought to him, not vice versa (2:18, 22). Afterward it is the man who speaks and makes a theological comment upon the woman's creation, not vice versa (2:23). It is the male who names the female, not vice versa (2:23).

Thus viewed from every possible angle, the whole narrative in Genesis 2 is the story of how God created the man and provided in every way for his well-being.... The other activities recorded in Genesis 2 are all relative to the man's existence, nature, and needs. This includes the creation of the woman. This chapter simply cannot be read in any other way.[24]

2. God created Adam first.

God created the man before He created the woman. Before Eve was formed, God placed Adam in the garden to care for it (2:15). Before Eve was formed, God brought the animals to Adam to be named (2:19). Before Eve was formed, God commanded Adam not to eat of the tree of the knowledge of good and evil lest he die (2:16, 17; most likely Adam taught Eve about God's command not to eat from the forbidden tree).

Adam was lord of the earth. Indeed, Adam was the human race, the first human. He represented the human race and it was embodied in him.

The creation priority of the man is not an incidental fact. Adam's prior creation has fundamental significance. We don't have to guess at this significance because the New Testament provides a divinely inspired commentary of Genesis 2. According to the principles of Bible interpretation, the Bible is its own best commentary. Scripture interprets Scripture. Thus, the same God who breathed out the words of Genesis 2 inspired Paul to comment on the true meaning of those words. Inspired by the Holy Spirit, Paul commented on Genesis 2 by writing, "I do not allow a woman to teach or exercise authority over a man, but to remain quiet. *For it was Adam who was first created*" (1 Tim. 2:12, 13*a*; italics added).

Thus, the New Testament uses the fact of Adam's prior creation to demonstrate that God designed the man to be the primary leader and teacher of the family of God. The leadership model provided in both the Old and New Testaments is that men primarily lead the people of God.

The same model is demonstrated historically on the worldwide level as well. Since the dawn of human civilization men, not women, have primarily ruled society.[25] Is this by chance? Or is it by design? Why are women seeking liberation and not vice versa? Genesis 2 provides the answer: from the beginning the Creator shaped the human clay in patriarchal form, not matriarchal or egalitarian form. Adam was the first patriarch.[26]

Adam's prior creation has fundamental significance. We don't have to guess at this significance because the New Testament provides a divinely inspired commentary of Genesis 2.

---

3. God formed the woman *out* of the man.

God created man and woman in amazingly different ways. God made the man out of the dust of the ground and breathed into him the breath of life (v. 7); God formed the woman out of the side of the man (v. 22). The woman's source of origin was the man. She was fashioned out of Adam's rib (v. 21). The woman's derivation from the man demonstrates not only equality in nature but also demonstrates role differences. How do we know this? The Bible tells us so.

According to the New Testament use of Genesis 2:22, the woman's origin from the man demonstrates the legitimacy of maintaining role differences between Christian men and women. In 1 Corinthians 11:8, Paul, citing

---

The New Testament uses the fact of Adam's prior creation to demonstrate that God designed the man to be the primary leader and teacher of the family of God.

Genesis 2:22, writes, "For man does not originate from woman, but woman from man." The points he seeks to prove from Genesis 2:22 are that the man "is the image and glory of God; but the woman is the glory of man," and also that "the man is the head of a woman" (1 Cor. 11:7, 3). The doctrine of headship and submission is rooted in the Genesis 2 story. The role distinctions Paul insists upon in his letters are based on Genesis 2.

4. God created the woman *for* the man.

If the first three points offend the modern sensibilities of equality, point four is totally unacceptable. Verse 18 reads: "Then the Lord God said, 'It is not good for the man to be alone; I will make him a helper suitable for him.'" God declared that Adam's singleness was not good. So God rectified the situation. He hand made "a helper suitable for him." Eve was not another male; she was not a clone of Adam nor was she a twin. She was similar but different.

She had her own biology, physiology, and psychology. She was made to complement the man, to help him populate and rule the earth, and to unite with him as a loving companion-partner. This is the first statement in the Bible concerning the woman's role; she is to be a help to the man.

A Help to the Man

The noun "helper" in Genesis 2:18 (Hebrew, *'ezer)* means "help," "support," "aid." It is *the key word used to describe the woman's role.* This is not a demeaning term. God is frequently described as a "help" to His people (Ps. 121). To be a helper means that the woman has the necessary ability, fitness, resources, and strength to be a help (see Prov. 31:10-31).

The woman was created for the man's sake, not vice versa (1 Cor. 11:9). Eve was created out of Adam's side (origin) and for him (goal). As one theologian reminds us: "The man's role is not defined in terms of the woman's, but the woman's in terms of the man's."[27] For the Christian man or woman, whatever God calls us to do or be is just, good, holy, and desirable. He is the Creator, and we are the clay. He instituted the leader-helper relationship between the first man and woman.

The Hebrew term for "suitable for him" (Hebrew, *kenegô)* means "like him," "corresponding-to-him," "matching him," "counterpart." Thus her nature corresponds to his. This shows their equality. She is not like the animals Adam names in verse 19. She, too, is an image bearer of God.

The New Testament commentary on Genesis 2:18 is 1 Corinthians 11:9: "for indeed man was not created for the woman's sake, but woman for the man's sake." Again Paul uses Genesis 2 to maintain sexual role distinctions. The fact that the woman was made *for* the sake of the man is proof that the man "is the image and glory of God; but the woman is the glory of man," and also that "the man is the head of a woman" (1 Cor. 11:7, 3).

This is the first statement in the Bible concerning the woman's role; she is to be a help to the man.

---

5. God gave the man the right to name the woman.

Before the Fall, Adam named his new companion. When Adam saw her, he said, "she shall be called woman" (Gen. 2:23). This is a generic name, not a personal name. After the Fall, Adam "called" his wife "Eve," a personal name (Gen. 3:20).

The one who names a thing or person has the authority and power to name (Gen. 1:5, 8, 10, 2:19, 20). For example, parents have the authority to name their children. The fact that Adam names the woman further suggests Adam's special authority role within the first couple's relationship.

6. God created the man and woman equal in nature.

God fashioned a partner for Adam out of his rib. This demonstrates their equality in nature. The man immediately recognized that the woman shared his same nature. So he said, "bone of my bones, and flesh of my flesh" (v. 23). She was not an inferior creature like the animals he had been busy naming (2:19, 20). She was taken out of his side and thus shared equally in his nature and in the bearing of the image of God.

C. Genesis 3: The Fall and the Battle of the Sexes

In Genesis 3, the man and woman sin against God. They disobey God's command and eat from "the tree of the knowledge of good and evil." Their disobedience and its resulting judgment is called the Fall. Genesis 3 "explains why men and women labor in toil, agony, and conflict all their days and why they die. Sin has wrought this dilemma, and nothing short of the removal of sin will end it."[28] All parties in the gender debate agree that the Fall changed male-female relations for the worse. Let us read the Genesis account of this event.

> **3:1** Now the serpent was more crafty than any beast of the field which the LORD God had made. And he said to the woman, "Indeed, has God said, 'You shall not eat from any tree of the garden'?"
>
> **3:6** When the woman saw that the tree was good for food, and that it was a delight to the eyes, and that the tree was desirable to make one wise, she took from its fruit and ate; and she gave also to her husband with her, and he ate.
>
> **3:9** Then the LORD God called to the man, and said to him, "Where are you?"
>
> **3:16** To the Woman He said, "I will greatly multiply Your pain in childbirth, In pain you shall bring forth children; Yet your desire will be for your husband, And he shall rule over you."

> **3:17** Then to Adam He said, "Because you have listened to the voice of your wife, and have eaten from the tree about which I commanded you, saying, 'You shall not eat from it'; Cursed is the ground because of you; In toil you shall eat of it All the days of your life."
>
> **3:19** "By the sweat of your face You will eat bread, Till you return to the ground, Because from it you were taken; For you are dust, And to dust you shall return."

Evangelical feminists insist that Genesis 3 is the first historical introduction of the concept of headship and submission. Genesis 2, they argue, teaches the full equality of the sexes, not headship and submission. A leading feminist spokesperson remarks, "It is only the result of the Fall (Genesis 3:16ff) that the woman becomes subordinate to man. There is not even a hint in the narrative of Genesis that woman is in any way subordinate to man prior to the Fall."[29]

Complementarians disagree. They insist that the concept is introduced in Genesis 2, as we have already shown, and that the Fall of Genesis 3 corrupted, rather than instituted, masculine leadership (headship). Let us consider three issues from the Genesis 3 account.

All parties in the gender debate agree that the Fall changed male-female relations for the worse.

---

1. Eve's deception.

It was not by chance that Satan appealed first to the woman rather than to the man. Like all master deceivers, Satan looked for the best way to sell his lies. Knowing God's creation design for the two sexes, he realized that the woman would be the more susceptible of the two to his subtle deceptions. He was right.

In verse 13, the woman herself frankly admits to God that Satan deceived her. So Satan struck at the woman first, attacking not only what God had said about the tree of the knowledge of good and evil, but also attacking God's order for the couple's relationship—she the helper, he the leader. German theologian Werner Neuer insightfully remarks, "The fall is therefore, not only the rebellion of mankind against God, but the setting aside of the divinely appointed order of male and female."[30]

2. Eve's penalty.

As a result of her sin, Eve would be afflicted with pain in her chief roles as mother and wife (v. 16). The first part of Eve's penalty for her transgression relates to her role as mother: "I will greatly multiply your pain in childbirth, In pain you shall bring forth children" (v. 16a).

The second part of Eve's penalty relates to her marital relationship: "Yet your desire will be for your husband, And he will rule over you." In general terms, these two pronouncements ("desire...rule") initiate what we call the battle of the sexes. The precise meaning of the "desire...rule" pronouncement on Eve is very difficult to interpret with certainty, especially the meaning of the word "desire."[31] Whatever the exact meaning of the "desire...rule" phrase, the man-woman relationship is distorted, and the woman is especially frustrated by the relationship.

Although these judgments will not be completely removed from the earth until the end, Cottrell is right in saying, "This does not mean, however, that we must accept them passively, any more than we must accept death passively. The atonement of Christ gives us the warrant to fight against these penal effects of sin in whatever ways we can."[32]

3. Adam's penalty.

God curses the ground because of Adam's sin. Only by misery and hard work will it yield food for sustaining life. "The woman's punishment struck at the deepest root of her being as wife and mother; the man's strikes at the innermost nerve of his life: his work, his activity, and provision for sustenance."[33]

Finally, and decisively, Adam will die and return to the ground. Eve, too, shares in Adam's death penalty. The reason for her inclusion in his judgment is that Adam is the appointed, representative head of the first family. His headship is recognized by the way in which, after the Fall, God called to Adam, not the woman, to respond to His summons, although the woman fell first (v. 9). Furthermore, Adam's headship is demonstrated by the way in which the couple is referred to as "the man and his wife" (v.8). In biblical language and God's governmental structure for the human race, Adam, the first man, was the head of the first family and ultimately of the whole human race (Rom. 5:12; 1 Cor. 15:22,45).

In summary, Genesis 1 and 2 reveal that men and women are created equally in the image of God but are different in function and relationship roles. The rest of the Old Testament illustrates these gender-based differences in a fallen world:

- The prominent leaders of the Old Testament are men: Noah, Abraham, Job, Isaac, Jacob, Joseph, Moses, Aaron, Joshua, Saul, Samuel, David, Solomon, Ezra, Nehemiah, Isaiah, Daniel, Ezekiel, and Jeremiah.
- Although priestesses were common in the religious practices of neighboring nations, Israel's priests were required to be male. It was not possible for a Hebrew woman to ever become a priestess. Israel had no female goddesses or priestesses and in this way was radically different from the surrounding nations.
- All of Israel's kings were male, except Athaliah, who violently usurped the throne.
- Almost all the leading national prophets were men, and we know of no women elders.

Women are not missing from the Old Testament history of God's covenant people, however. Women prayed directly to God with great effectiveness, offered sacrifices to Him through the priests, and walked in intimate relationship with Him. Throughout the Old Testament, we read of many godly, heroic, influential women—women of amazing strength, wisdom, and competence. Although God makes His covenant with Abraham, for example, Sarah is a leading player in the story. Rebekah, Rachel, and Leah stand as prominent women alongside their patriarchal husbands. Although real love and devotion are demonstrated between these couples, there is also cruelty and manipulation.

The primary role of the woman in the Old Testament was that of mother and wife. The high status of a wife and mother is praised in Proverbs 31:10: "An excellent wife, who can find? For her worth is far above jewels." In some cases, women served in more public, national roles. For example, some women served at the "doorway of the tent of meeting" (Ex. 38:8), and some were prophetesses. Deborah was a prophetess and also a judge of Israel.[34] Among the women of Israel, Miriam was a leader and prophetess.

The Old Testament doesn't paint a romantic or idealistic picture of the treatment of women. It paints a realistic portrait. The Old Testament shows the cruelty of polygamy and the king's harem. We find examples of a double standard in sexual conduct (Gen. 38:11-26) under which men divorced their wives unjustly, but wives couldn't divorce their husbands. God hated their action and strongly condemned it through the prophet Malachi (Mal. 2:13-16). Summarizing the situation, Werner Neuer gives a balanced conclusion:

All these examples show that the undervaluation of women and discrimination against them in the Old Testament had not been fully overcome. Despite this, one must admit in the light of the mass of Old Testament evidence for the high valuation placed on women that (as Doller concludes) "Without doubt the woman in Israel had a status found among few other peoples."[35]

With the foundation of Old Testament teaching securely under us, we are now ready to investigate the New Testament teaching on gender roles.

Questions

1. List several reasons why our study begins in Genesis.
2. Do you believe that the Genesis account records accurate history and truth? Explain your answer.
3. What significant truths are taught in Genesis 1:26-28? Why are these truths vitally important to our study?
4. What do evangelical feminists believe Genesis 2 teaches concerning men and women?
5. How would you answer someone who says that Adam's creation prior to Eve is irrelevant to the gender debate?
6. What does the statement, "Scripture interprets Scripture," mean? Why is this principle of interpretation ("Scripture interprets Scripture") especially important to our study?
7. Using Genesis 1:26-28 and 2:7-24, describe the activities God expected of the woman He created.
8. Using Genesis 2:7-24, describe the ways in which Adam and Eve were created equal.
9. What specific details in the Genesis 2 story demonstrate that Adam is to be the leader of the first couple?
10. What is meant by the term "the Fall"? Why is a belief in the Fall of the human race (Genesis 3) absolutely essential if we are to correctly understand gender problems and solutions?
11. In your own words, explain the meaning of the statement, "Adam, the first man, was the head of the first family and ultimately of the whole human race (see Romans 5:12; 1 Cor. 15:22,45).
12. According to the Old Testament, what leadership positions were restricted to men only?
13. What impact does the cross of Jesus Christ have on God's design for men and women? Explain your answer.
14. What did you learn from this chapter that will help shape your thinking and actions?

II. Jesus Christ Appointed Male Leadership for His Church

"I sure didn't realize that Genesis was so vital to our topic. What do we study next, Paul and his epistles?" Tom asks.

"No, we'll next look directly at Jesus Christ, specifically His own male gender and His choice of twelve male apostles."

"Do you really think these two issues are significant?"

"Tom, 'Jesus is Lord' is the confession of every Christian. So, for a Christian, no one is more important to the gender debate than Jesus Christ. The fact that Jesus was born a male and prayerfully chose twelve male apostles to officially represent Him is monumentally significant."

"Some of my professors say that Jesus' maleness and choice of male apostles doesn't mean anything theologically. They say that such choices were necessary because the first-century Jewish culture didn't allow women to preach and lead. So Jesus had to concede to the standards of society."

"What an insult to Jesus! The Jesus of the Gospels was absolutely courageous. He was unafraid to give new, radical teaching to His tradition-bound culture. Jesus didn't give in to sinful culture or let women down at this critical moment in history."

"Good point!"

"Tom, Jesus Christ gave His Church male leadership. His male gender and His deliberate choice of twelve male apostles were based on Genesis 2, God's original creation design for the sexes."

"I guess that does make them significant points."

"Yes it does. In fact, it cannot be denied that these two facts have impacted Christ's followers for the past two thousand years. The impact is still evident today among hundreds of millions of Roman Catholics, Orthodox, many in the Anglican Communion, and conservative Protestant churches that require male leadership for their churches. So let's explore Jesus' maleness and choice of male apostles."

—❧—

A. Jesus Had to Be a Man

Jesus Christ has two natures, a fully divine nature and a fully human nature. Yet He is one person. As fully human, Jesus Christ had to be either male or female. He assumed a male human nature and came into the world as the Son of God, not the daughter of God.

Evangelical feminists claim that Jesus' maleness was necessary for practical reasons. His first-century culture would not have allowed Him to preach and lead if He had been a woman, they say. What is essential to their theological position is that Jesus is fully human. His gender, they claim, is theologically irrelevant although it was a practical necessity.

Feminist Views of Jesus' Maleness

Rebecca Groothuis writes: "For historical and cultural reasons, it was necessary that God be incarnated as a male human. But because God is neither male nor female and is imaged in woman and man equally, it was not theologically necessary for God Incarnate to be male."[36] She goes on to say, "To impute a theological significance and necessity to Christ's maleness is to put into reasonable question the efficacy of Christ's redemptive work on behalf of women."[37]

Similarly, Aída Besanfon Spencer, professor of New Testament at Gordon-Conwell Theological Seminary, states: "Although God became a male, God primarily became a human; otherwise, in some way males would be more saved than females."[38]

Jesus' maleness was not incidental, however. His male gender was biblically and theologically necessary. The Bible is not silent about His gender nor is it silent about the requirements for His gender. Jesus had to be not only human, but a male human—a first-born, Jewish male from a certain tribe and family. As to Jesus' maleness, Cottrell writes, "This is a fact affirmed from the beginning of the Bible to its end, from the masculine seed of woman in Genesis 3:15 to the bridegroom in Revelation 21."[39]

According to God's plan of salvation, Jesus Christ is the counterpart to Adam, not Eve. As one theologian writes, "Both Adam and Christ entered the world through a special act of God. Both entered the world sinless; both acted on behalf of those who God considered in them representatively....

Adam as the husband of Eve is also a type of the Bridegroom in relation to the church as the bride."[40]

The New Testament calls Adam a "type" of Christ (Rom. 5:14). The word type in this usage means "a symbol or figure of something to come," such as an Old Testament person or event that prefigures (or foreshadows) a New Testament person or event. Adam, for example, prefigures Christ. Jesus is the "last Adam" and "the second man" (1 Cor. 15:45, 47). The first Adam failed; the last Adam did not fail. Like Adam, Jesus is the head of a race, a new humanity. Thus to deny the necessity of Christ's maleness in regard to God's salvation plan is to distort that plan. Feminist efforts to deny the necessity of Christ's maleness promote serious doctrinal error.

The requirement for a male redeemer is not unlike other biblical requirements. For example, Jesus taught that "salvation is from the Jews" (John 4:22). Jesus thus had to be a Jew. He also had to be a first-born son from the genealogical

---
Jesus had to be not only human, but a male human.
---

line of Abraham and David, rightful heir to the promises of God, the true seed. He had to be the true King, not the queen, of Israel; the Lord, not the lady, of the universe; the kinsman-redeemer; bridegroom; and perfect male Passover Lamb of God.

"The Bible's overwhelming emphasis on the maleness of Christ, as it assigns to him exclusively male titles and roles, shows unequivocally that it was God's intentional plan to redeem the world not just through a human being but through a human being who is male.... That he continues to relate to us in male roles shows that his gender was not just a cultural accommodation."[41]

Furthermore, Jesus Christ is the fullest revelation of God. He is God in flesh. Thus He had to be male. The God of the Bible *reveals and defines Himself* in Holy Scripture in almost exclusively masculine language, titles, offices, images, and roles. This is not a cultural accident; female deities were numerous in the patriarchal cultures of the ancient Near East and Mediterranean world. Here are some examples: the Egyptian goddess Isis, one of the most important deities in the Mediterranean world; the Canaanite goddess Asherah; the Babylonian goddess Ishtar; the Greek goddesses Artemis and Aphrodite (Roman Venus); the Roman queen goddess Juno. A female deity was not offensive to the people in the ancient world of the Bible. Thus Jesus' maleness was not a cultural accommodation. Rather, Judaism and Christianity were unique in the ancient world because of their monotheism and exclusive masculine description of God.

The God of the Bible is always *He,* never *She.* He is Father, *never* Mother. The triune God of the Bible is Lord, King, Master, Husband, Kinsman-Redeemer, and the Father of our Lord Jesus Christ. Jesus Christ taught His followers to call God their "Father." He taught them to pray, "Our Father who is in heaven," not "Our Mother who is in heaven." God the Father is not merely like a father, He is *the* Father; Jesus Christ is not merely like a son, He is *the* Son. These names cannot be changed simply because people

---
The God of the Bible is always He, never She.
---

are offended by them. The biblical record testifies to the truth that, as God incarnate and chief revealer of God, Jesus had to be male.

Finally, if there is any doubt in your mind about the necessity of Jesus' maleness, listen to the apostle Paul, who was personally chosen and commissioned by Christ to speak for Him to the Gentile world: "But I do not allow a woman to teach or exercise authority over a man, but to remain quiet. For it was Adam who was first created, and then Eve" (1 Tim. 2:12, 13). Note also his inspired teaching in 1 Corinthians 11:3, "Christ is the head of every man, and the man is the head of a woman, and God is the head of Christ." Furthermore, he declares that the man "is the image and glory of God; but the woman is the glory of man" (1 Cor. 11:7).

Jesus could not be a woman because, as a woman, He could not exercise authority over male disciples. According to God's creation design of the male-female relationship, the male partner is invested with the headship-representative-authority role. Thus the head of the Church is Jesus Christ, a man.

No Goddess for God's People

God could have limited descriptions of Himself to impersonal gender-neutral terms like Rock, Fire, Holy One, Living One, etc. He didn't; He is a personal being and He seeks relationship with those who are created in His image.

There are a few instances in the Bible where feminine imagery is used to describe God (Deut. 32:18; Isa. 49:14, 15, 66:13). But most of these take the form of a simile, a figure of speech in which a comparison is made between two distinct things that are not otherwise alike.

For example, Isaiah 42:14 states, "Now like a woman in labor I will groan."

In this case, God's crying out to His people is compared to the crying out of a woman in labor. The verse doesn't state or imply that God is a woman in labor or that He is feminine. The same kind of imagery is also employed by men in the Bible. Moses and Paul, for example, use the imagery of a woman giving birth or of a nursing mother to describe their work and feelings (Gal. 4:19; 1 Thess. 2:7; Num. 11:12, cf.; John 16:21, 22). Jesus also compares His desire for His people to that of a hen gathering her chicks (Matt. 23:37). These comparisons, however, do not indicate that these men are women. William Mouser is absolutely correct when he states: "There is no Goddess in the Bible."[42]

B. Jesus Appointed Twelve Male Apostles

During His earthly ministry, Jesus Christ personally trained and appointed twelve men whom He called "apostles" (Luke 6:13). Before choosing the Twelve, Jesus spent the entire night in prayer to His Father. Read the following verses from Luke 6:

> **6:12** It was at this time that He went off to the mountain to pray, and He spent the whole night in prayer to God.

> **6:13** And when day came, He called His disciples to Him and chose twelve of them, whom He also named as apostles.

Apostles of Jesus Christ

The term *apostle* was first used by our Lord to describe twelve uniquely chosen disciples, also called the Twelve (Luke 6:13). The Greek word *apostolos* is literally "one who is sent-out." In this case, Jesus Christ is the sender, and the Twelve are the sent ones (they are not volunteers); they are His official ambassadors, emissaries, envoys, or message bearers. They are Christ's authoritative representatives and interpreters, His accredited teachers—inspired, guided, and protected by the Holy Spirit. While He was with them on earth, Jesus said to His apostles: "I have many more things to say to you, but you cannot bear them now. But when He, the Spirit of truth, comes, He will guide you into

> all the truth" (John 16:12, 13a; also 14:25, 26, 15:26, 27; Acts 1:1-3).
>   Because the apostles speak Christ's words by the power of the Holy Spirit, John can say without pride or self-deception, "he who knows
>
> God [the true believer] listens to us [apostles]; he who is not from God does not listen to us. By this we know the spirit of truth and the spirit of error" (1 John 4:6).

In perfect obedience and submission to His Father's will, Jesus chose twelve males to be His apostles. Thus these men were also God the Father's choice. Jesus' choice of male apostles was based on earnest prayer, divine Old Testament principles, and God the Father's guidance. His choice was not based on His fear of first-century, male-dominated culture.

Even after Christ's ascension into heaven, when a replacement for Judas, one of the Twelve, became necessary, only men (Acts 1:21) were considered. Of the two men who qualified, Joseph and Matthias, one was chosen for that position by the risen Lord Jesus Christ Himself through the means of the lot. Two years later, the risen Christ appeared to the man Saul on the Damascus Road and appointed him as the chief apostle to the Gentiles.

How could anyone honestly read the life of Jesus Christ and think that Jesus accommodated His choice of male apostles to the sinful, male chauvinistic spirit of His age?

Despite His divinely guided choice of twelve male apostles, feminist teachers claim that Jesus' selection of twelve males was a necessary concession to the patriarchal culture of His day. A leading feminist apologist writes, "Isn't it possible that excluding women from the Twelve was another concession to first-century culture—as well as to decorum?"[43]

But how could anyone honestly read the life of Jesus Christ and think that Jesus accommodated His choice of male apostles to the sinful, male chauvinistic spirit of His age? The facts do not agree with the feminists' portrayal of Jesus. Consider the ways in which Jesus is portrayed in Scripture.

1. Jesus was fearless.
Jesus Christ did not fear the religious establishment. In unprecedented ways He exposed its hypocrisy. He called the professional scribes and Pharisees

blind guides, pompous fools, sanctimonious frauds, robbers of widows, money lovers, double-talkers, false teachers, perverts, murderers of the prophets, serpents, brood of vipers, and hell-bound, self-righteous, self-deceived hypocrites (Matt. 23). Twice, at great risk to His life, Jesus acted as reformer by driving the moneychangers out of the temple court with a whip. He accused the priests of forsaking their spiritual duties and exploiting the people for their own financial profit.

Jesus Christ did not accommodate His teachings or actions to sinful, man-made traditions. Jesus claimed that His teachings and ways were like "new wine" that required "fresh wineskins." The old wineskin of external, legalistic, rabbinic Judaism was unable to contain His fresh, new teachings without bursting apart (Matt. 9:17). Directed by the Holy Spirit, and bolder than any Old Testament prophet, Jesus did not hesitate to rebuke traditions that contradicted or superseded God's Holy Word (Mark 7:1-23). Repeatedly He defied legalistic Sabbath traditions, declaring Himself to be Lord of the Sabbath. For these acts, the religious establishment believed that Jesus deserved death.

One of the reasons Jesus was hated and eventually crucified was because He consistently violated certain rabbinic traditions. Yet, despite His attacks on man-made traditions, even His fiercest enemies had to admit that Jesus spoke the truth. He feared and showed partiality to no one: "Teacher, we know that You are truthful and teach the way of God in truth, and defer to no one; for You are not partial to any" (Matt. 22:16).

2. Jesus was a non-traditionalist.

The volume of new teachings that Jesus presented to the tradition-bound people of first-century Israel is truly remarkable. Jesus' teachings and actions toward women were new and quite untraditional. The Jesus of the Gospels was not afraid to challenge male traditions nor the hard-headed defenders of male-centered tradition. No wonder the people said, "What is this? A new teaching with authority!" (Mark 1:27b). Consider the following:

- In the oft-quoted *Sermon on the Mount,* Jesus repeatedly declared "You have heard that it was said [in the ancient traditions]...but I say to you" (Matt. 5:21-48). One of the traditions Jesus rebuked was the prized male tradition of divorce. Many Jewish men in Christ's time thought that the Law allowed them to divorce their wives for any reason as long as they provided the wife a certificate of divorce. Jesus, however, abolished their divorce tradition.

With absolute authority, He renewed the original design of faithful, monogamous marriage and restricted the grounds for divorce to one cause only: marital unfaithfulness (Matt. 5:31, 32; 19:3, 9).

• In the same sermon, Jesus also said, "You have heard that it was said you shall not commit adultery;' but I say to you that everyone who looks at a woman with lust for her has already committed adultery with her in his heart" (Matt. 5:27, 28). Superficial, self-serving, religious men could feel self-righteous because they had never committed the physical act of adultery. But Jesus warned them that lustful looks or thinking about a woman for self-satisfying sexual pleasure reveals an immoral, adulterous heart and that such men are guilty before God. Jesus thus challenged many of the religious leaders' longstanding attitudes and their cherished male chauvinistic traditions.

• The manner in which Jesus interacted with women was no less radical. To the shock of His twelve disciples and the woman herself, Jesus broke all social customs when He spoke at length to a Samaritan woman about divine truths and her spiritual and moral condition (John 4:9. 27). Through her testimony, many came to Jesus and believed.

• Twice, Jesus publicly commended Mary, the sister of Lazarus, for her spiritual priorities and insight—once for choosing to sit at His feet to hear His words rather than be distracted by excessive meal preparations (Luke 10:42) and once for anointing Him for burial when everyone else around her totally misunderstood the sacredness of the moment (John 12:1-8).

• At times, a band of loyal women accompanied Jesus on His travels and cared for His physical needs (Luke 8:1-3). These women loved the Lord Jesus and wanted to be with Him and serve Him. He welcomed their ministry.

• Mary Magdalene and several other women had the distinct honor of being the first people to see Jesus Christ after His resurrection. He also entrusted them to announce His resurrection to His disciples and to communicate to them His plans for meeting with them. John's account of the meeting between Mary Magdalene and Jesus after His resurrection is one of the most touching stories in the New Testament (John 20:1-18).

• Jesus' overarching, fundamental command for life in the community of the risen Lord is to "love one another, even as I have loved you" (John 13:34). Selfless, self-sacrificing Christian love heals the war of the sexes. "Through his absolute love command...he throws out once and for all every kind of male egoism or oppression of women.... Jesus shows the only way in which the relationship between the sexes, a relationship that has been upset by sin, can be healed."[44]

The volume of new teachings that Jesus presented to the tradition-bound people of first-century Israel is truly remarkable. Jesus' teachings and actions toward women were new and quite untraditional. The Jesus of the Gospels was not afraid to challenge male traditions nor the hard-headed defenders of male-centered tradition.

---

3. Jesus didn't fail women.

During His life on earth, Jesus honored, defended, and elevated women in remarkable new ways. He did not fear the male chauvinist authorities of His day. Even so, He chose twelve male apostles. Why? The answer to this question is extremely important.

Evangelical feminists say that the time wasn't right for the appointment of female apostles. They contend that first-century culture required Jesus to appoint male apostles although in theory He would approve of women apostles. According to feminist interpreters, God had to adapt His Word to the prevailing patriarchal culture of the Old Testament in order to be understood and accepted.[45] Thus, when the Messiah finally came as God in the flesh, God once again cowered before the dreaded monster of patriarchal culture. Feminist interpreters believe that Jesus Christ could not offend patriarchal culture by appointing a female apostle. According to this view, even Jesus Christ could not break loose from Genesis 3 and the curse!

The Bible, however, says that Jesus came into the world and specifically into a Jewish culture at God's appointed time and place (Gal.4:4). So that was the time to act, and Jesus was the only person with the power and authority to appoint women apostles, if such were possible. If He did not speak out then, when would be the right time to speak out? When would society be ready for female apostles? Would it be in A.D. 1848 at the first women's rights conference, the Seneca Falls Convention at Seneca Falls, New York? Would it be in A.D. 1949 with the appearance of Simone de Beauvoir's book, *The Second Sex?* Would Western secular society determine the appropriate time for Jesus to speak?

If Jesus, through His work of redemption, intended to abolish role distinctions as feminists claim, then the choosing of the Twelve was the crucial moment in history to act and appoint women to the apostolate. The apostolate was the foundational office of the Church, and Jesus' choice of the twelve apostles affected the Church for the next two thousand years. So the choosing of the Twelve was the opportune time to break with Israel's patriarchal leadership structure. But Jesus made no such break. He continued the pattern of male leadership.

Jesus (and the Father) were well aware of the long-term consequences of this choice. The twelve apostles form a link with the twelve sons of Jacob, the twelve tribes of Israel (Rev. 21:12-14).[46] To appoint twelve men was to continue with the male leadership of the past. It was also to project male leadership into the future because the twelve male apostles will be named and forever remembered on the foundation stones of the new eternal city of Jerusalem (Rev. 21:14).

If Jesus is the supreme egalitarian that some wish Him to be, He surely failed women at a critical moment in history. As the hailed liberator of women, should not Jesus have chosen six women and six men apostles, or at the very least, one female apostle? Could not a woman apostle have ministered to women?

Finally, we must ask, why would Jesus need to worry about rejection for choosing women apostles when He was already rejected because of His scandalous teachings and behavior? Cottrell observes that Jesus "was neither listened to nor respected anyway by those who would have objected to such a choice. If he declined to appoint a woman to the Twelve just for this reason, then the strategy was futile and a golden opportunity wasted."[47]

No matter how they try to phrase it, feminists ultimately insult Jesus Christ's character when they claim that the absence of female apostles is due to

---

**If Jesus, through His work of redemption,
intended to abolish role distinctions as feminists
claim, then the choosing of the Twelve was the
crucial moment in history to act and appoint women
to the apostolate.**

His concession to first-century Jewish customs. If Jesus caved in to His male chauvinistic culture in the choice of apostolic leadership, what He did and said about women becomes largely irrelevant. We can count Him out of the gender debate. But this is not the case. Jesus acted on divine principles (Genesis 2) in His appointment of male apostles. He is the solution to gender confusion:

> Jesus Christ came to show the right way, the way of co-operation, not competition, the way of peace, not war, between the sexes. He did not come to change the created order, which includes the headship of men and the submission of women; but rather to transform it by his love and grace, so that what God created can be redeemed and function properly. If we don't find this way, then both men and women will be the losers, and the truth will be hidden from the world.[48]

Questions

1. For a Christian, why is Jesus Christ central to the gender debate? List as many reasons as possible.

2. What do Christians mean when they say Jesus Christ has two natures, yet is one person?

3. List several reasons why Jesus Christ had to be born a male human. Which reason do you consider to be most important?

4. Why would denying the necessity of Jesus' male gender conflict with God's plan of salvation? Be specific.

5. How would you answer someone who claims that we can pray and address God as Mother as well as Father?

6. What does the term *apostle* mean? What significance is attached to being an apostle?

7. List theological and/or biblical reasons why Jesus chose male apostles only.

8. Give one example from Jesus' non-traditional **actions** toward women that most impressed you. Explain why you chose this example.

9. Give one example from Jesus' non-traditional **teachings** regarding men and or women that most impressed you. Explain why you chose this example.

10. What major teaching of Jesus Christ, if followed, should end all male abuse of women?

11. Cite one example of Jesus' courage and fearlessness in the face of religious opposition. In light of this example, how would you respond to someone who said that Jesus' appointment of male apostles is merely an accommodation to the prevailing customs of His day?

12. Explain why the following statement is true: "The choosing of the twelve was the crucial moment in history to act and appoint women to the apostolate."

13. In what ways is the feminist answer to Christ's maleness and choice of male apostles an insult to the character of Christ? List more than one reason.

14. What did you learn from this chapter that will help shape your thinking and actions related to the gender debate?

III. Through His Apostles, Jesus Christ Gave Instruction on Marriage

This study gets more intriguing the deeper we dig into it," Tom exclaims.
"Yes. As the Scottish writer, Thomas Carlyle, said, 'the Bible is full of infinities and immensities.' The more you study the Bible, the more you will see how truly profound it is, and that its author is God. In fact, we've only begun to scratch the surface of our topic."

"What's next?" Tom wants to know.

"Christian marriage."

"I thought we already looked at Jesus' instruction on marriage in Matthew 19," Tom says.

"True, but Jesus gave further, in-depth teaching on Christian marriage through His apostles."

"What do you mean, through His apostles?"

"After His ascension into heaven, Jesus continued His work and teaching through His apostles. Although Jesus left behind no documents written by His hand, He supernaturally empowered the apostles to proclaim His teachings and to reproduce them in written form. So to reject the apostles' letters is to reject Jesus Christ. To disobey the apostles is to disobey Jesus Christ."

"I didn't realize that," Tom says with surprise.

"Tom, the apostles Peter and Paul provide us with Jesus' complete teaching on Christian marriage. Both apostles teach equality in marriage, masculine headship, and the woman's submission."

"Man, do people hate the word submission! To believe that a wife should submit to her husband fires up intense emotional debate at school."

"I know. Nevertheless, it's still a Christian doctrine that is repeatedly stated and defended by the apostles."

"Yes, I know it's in Scripture," Tom responds, "but maybe it's all cultural, and not relevant for us today."

"It's not that simple. Both Paul and Peter feel strongly about this issue. Paul, more than Peter, adamantly argues for marital headship and submission.

He defends his position with powerful arguments from the Old Testament creation accounts, the model of Christ and the Church, the relationship of the members of the Trinity, a command of Christ, and his own apostolic authority."

"Wow! I didn't realize that," Tom remarks.

"Let's study the core passages. As we proceed, note very carefully the meaning of the key words the apostles use to define the structure of Christian marriage. Tom, words are important. When communicating doctrinal truth not just any word will do. Note also that changing the meaning of a word changes the doctrine it is intended to communicate. And there's one more thing. Don't miss what the apostles say about the role of the husband, particularly his Christlike love for his wife. Don't allow the debate over submission to cause you to miss what the New Testament says about the husband's self-sacrificing love for his wife."

A. 1 Peter 3:1-7: Submission and Understanding

Peter was one of the twelve apostles. He lived with Jesus Christ, heard Him teach, conversed with Him, and watched His daily interaction with men and women. Jesus Christ directly commissioned Peter to be a witness to His life and teachings, to be one of the foundation-layers of His Church. As such, Peter's letters are authoritative and irreplaceable. Peter teaches us what Jesus Christ taught him, thus it is our duty to practice and teach what is contained in these inspired letters.

What did Jesus Christ teach about the husband-wife relationship? The following instruction from the letter of 1 Peter, chapter 3 is clear:

3:1 In the same way, you wives, be submissive to your own husbands so that even if any of them are disobedient to the word, they may be won without a word by the behavior of their wives,

3:2 as they observe your chaste and respectful behavior.

3:3 Your adornment must not be merely external—braiding the hair, and wearing gold jewelry, or putting on dresses;

3:4 but let it be the hidden person of the heart, with the imperishable quality of a gentle and quiet spirit, which is precious in the sight of God.

3:5 For in this way in former times the holy women also, who hoped in God, used to adorn themselves, being submissive to their own husbands;

3:6 just as Sarah obeyed Abraham, calling him lord, and you have become her children if you do what is right without being frightened by any fear.

3:7 You husbands in the same way, live with your wives in an understanding way, as with someone weaker, since she is a woman; and show her honor as a fellow heir of the grace of life, so that your prayers will not be hindered.

1. Peter instructs Christian wives to submit to their husbands.

The theme of the entire section of the letter in which this passage appears is submission (2:11-3:12). Starting in chapter 2, Peter instructs his beloved readers to "submit yourselves for the Lord's sake to every human institution" (2:13). Peter applies this exhortation to civil government (2:13, 14), servant-master relations (2:18-20), and wives to husbands (3:1-6). Thus submission to authority is a Christian virtue; it is not just a woman's issue. "Men as well as women," writes Clark, "should be submissive in their subordinate relationships."[49]

Peter offers specific instruction to Christian wives: "you wives, be submissive to your own husbands so that if any of them are disobedient to the word, they may be won without a word by the behavior of their wives." Peter's exhortation to submit is not solely for wives with non-Christian husbands. Notice that he says, "if any" are non-Christians. Many, if not most, husbands would be Christians, but "if any" are not Christians, Peter says to win them through distinctive Christian behavior. The reciprocal responsibilities listed for Christian husbands in verse 7 shows that Christian husbands are also in view. So, whether or not a woman has a Christian husband, she is to "be submissive" to her husband.

a. The meaning of submission *(hypotassō)*

The Greek word for *be submissive* is one of four key words central to the gender debate:

- Help/helper   (Hebrew, *'ezer*)
- Be submissive   (Greek, *hypotassō*)
- Head   (Greek, *kephalē*)
- Exercise authority   (Greek, *authenteō*)

It is essential to understand all four terms.

The Greek verb for "be submissive" is *hypotassō*. It means "submit to," "be subject to," "be subordinate to." The word always implies a relationship of submission to an authority.

In our contemporary, secularized culture, to apply the "S" word—submission—to the husband-wife relationship is to label oneself a chauvinist or Neanderthal. Many people imagine womanly submission in terms of cavemen dragging women around by the hair, or of society regressing into the Dark Ages. The word can hardly be used in our culture without misunderstanding and strong disdain. It is loaded with negative, provocative connotations, yet submission is a biblical word and a Christian virtue. We cannot avoid it.

Evangelical feminists know that submission is a Christian virtue, but they advocate "mutual submission" between husband and wife. They deny any unique, God-appointed, authority role reserved for the husband. They are highly offended by the idea that the wife has a special duty to submit to her husband and vigorously deny that a Christian wife must submit to her husband in a way in which he is not called to submit to her.

The problem, however, is that the Greek word used for *submission* means "submission to an authority." Peter means what he says, and he chooses the right word to communicate what he wants to say. Wayne Grudem, professor of theology at Trinity Evangelical Divinity School and a leading scholar for the complementarian position, says that the Greek term for *submission* "is never 'mutual' in its force; it is always one-directional in its reference to submission to an authority."[50] Even more precisely, Grudem points out that "in every example we can find, when person A is said to 'be subject to' person B, person B has a unique authority which person A does not have."[51] Note the following examples from the New Testament:

- Jesus subject to His parents (Luke 2:51)
- Citizens subject to government (Rom. 13:1)
- Demons subject to the disciples (Luke 10:17)
- Universe subject to Christ (1 Cor. 15:27)
- The Church subject to Christ (Eph. 5:24)
- Unseen, heavenly authorities subject to Christ (1 Peter 3:22)
- Believers subject to God (James 4:7)
- Believers subject to their spiritual leaders (1 Cor. 16:15, 16)

- Christ subject to God the Father (1 Cor. 15:28)
- Servants subject to masters (Titus 2:5)
- Wives subject to husbands (Eph. 5:23)

Please note that none of these relationships is ever reversed. Among these headship-submission relationships, masters are not subject to servants, government is not subject to citizens, Christ is not subject to angels, parents are not subject to children, and husbands are not subject to wives. The New Testament never commands the husband to submit to his wife; it is always the reverse. In Christian marriage, husband-wife roles (leader/helper) are not interchangeable nor are they irrelevant.

The word *submission* can hardly be used in our culture without misunderstanding and strong disdain. It is loaded with negative, provocative connotations, yet submission is a biblical word and a Christian virtue. We cannot avoid it.

Keep in mind that there are different kinds of subordination relationships, each of which requires a different response on the part of both the subordinate and the head. The husband-wife relationship is not a boss-employee, a commander-soldier, or a teacher-student relationship. It is a love relationship, the most intimate of all human relationships. It is a covenant-marriage relationship in which two adults become united as one. Within this union, one partner lovingly takes the lead and the other willingly and actively supports that lead. According to Genesis 2, the wife's role is to affirm the husband in his leadership. *This is an active, not passive, role. It requires wisdom, social skill, insight, love, and strength.* For a biblical example of this active, positive role of helper, read Proverbs 31:10-31.

Since the marriage relationship consists of both oneness and role differences, a great deal of mutuality and interdependence will exist (see especially 1 Cor.7:3-5; 11:11, 12). "Within a healthy Christian marriage...there will be large elements of mutual consultation and seeking of wisdom, and most decisions will come by consensus between husband and wife."[52] The marriage partners are to complement each other, not to compete against each other.

> **Key Word:** *Submission* **(Greek,** *hypotassō)*
>
> In the context of the husband-wife relationship, the word *submission (hypotassō)* means "submit to," "be subject to," "be subordinate to." The word implies a relationship of submission to an authority. As Grudem explains, the verb *hypotassō "is* never 'mutual' in its force; it is always one-directional in its reference to submission to an authority."[53] He further comments, " In every example we can find, when person A is said to 'be subject to' person B, person B has a unique authority which person A does not have."[54] The New Testament never says the husband is to submit to the wife; it is always the reverse. The term itself does not suggest "mutual" submission.

b. The inner beauty of a submissive spirit

In stark contrast to secular society's intolerance and contempt for the word *submission,* Peter says that the wife's submission to her husband is of true, lasting beauty in God's eyes. The beauty that God admires in a wife is a "gentle and quiet spirit" and "being submissive" to one's husband (vv. 4, 5). These precious qualities stem from the wife's faith in God, not the fear of her husband or society (vv. 5, 6).

In contrast to her inner, spiritual beauty, Peter warns Christian wives to avoid being overly concerned about external, physical beauty. He addresses concerns regarding clothing, hair styles, jewelry, and cosmetics by writing, "Your adornment must not be merely external—braiding the hair, and wearing gold jewelry, or putting on dresses." Peter isn't saying a woman can't wear a dress or braid her hair. What he says is, a Christian wife should be supremely concerned about her inner beauty, her true character, her inner attitudes, her real self, or "the hidden person of the heart" rather than her external dress, which is often unduly emphasized.

c. Limits on submission

In the context of the Christian community and the New Testament, submission and headship describe how the man-woman relationship is structured (Genesis 2, leader/helper) and what the disposition of the woman should be toward her husband. The Christian husband is never told to force submission on his wife. Rather, the Christian wife voluntarily helps and submits to her husband's leadership because she believes it to be God's design for her in the relationship.

> **Şince the marriage relationship consists of both oneness and role differences, a great deal of mutuality and interdependence will exist.**

Furthermore, a Christian wife's submission to her husband is not mindless, blind, slavish submission. Such submission is not beautiful. It is a perverted, pagan concept of submission that has dehumanized women worldwide. Christian marital submission does not mean that:

- The wife is inferior
- The wife is to be passive or surrender all independent thought
- The husband is to stifle a wife's creativity, gifts, or individuality
- The wife is to do everything the husband demands or that the husband is to oppress the wife
- The wife is to enable the husband's sin and irresponsibility
- The wife is to live with a psychologically dangerous or abusive man

Biblical submission doesn't eliminate the biblical principles of justice, fairness, love, kindness, and compassion that every Christian—female as well as male—should practice in every aspect of life and marriage. Peter closes his exhortations on submission (1 Peter 2:13-3:7) with these words, which apply also to marriage, "To sum up, all of you be harmonious, sympathetic, brotherly, kindhearted, and humble in spirit; not returning evil for evil or insult for insult, but giving a blessing instead; for you were called for the very purpose that you might inherit a blessing" (3:8, 9). This is wonderful marital counsel for both husbands and wives.

It is also important to remember that no husband has absolute authority, only Christ does. It should go without saying that a wife doesn't submit to a husband's evil demands or sinful schemes (Acts 5:1-10). A wife has a biblical duty to confront her husband's sin (Matt. 18:15) and to admonish him (Col. 3:16). She can't be his God-given helper (Gen. 2:18) if she doesn't correct him, but her attitude in confronting and admonishing is that of a loving, submissive partner. Under certain heartbreaking circumstances, a Christian wife may even to have divorce or live apart from a wicked husband (Matt. 19:9).

A case in point: Peter assumes that a Christian wife with a pagan husband has the freedom and obligation to think and believe differently than her husband. She is to seek to persuade her husband to believe in Christ. Jesus Christ is Lord, thus a wife's loyalty is first and foremost to Him, not to her husband. Peter says a Christian wife must "do what is right" and not be frightened even by a hostile husband (v. 6). A Christian wife with a non-Christian husband will have to graciously and wisely refuse to worship her husband's false god or believe his false doctrines.

Biblical submission doesn't eliminate the biblical principles of justice, fairness, love, kindness, and compassion that every Christian—female as well as male—should practice in every aspect of life and marriage.

---

2. Peter supports submission with the Old Testament Scriptures.

Peter's teaching on submission is not a concession to the prevailing Greco-Roman marital customs. Nor does he rely upon Greco-Roman ethical rules or stoic philosophy. Instead, he follows Christ's example of Bible interpretation. Just as Jesus used the Genesis account on marriage to teach the ideal pattern for marriage (Matt. 19:4-8), Peter uses the Genesis account to support his teaching on submission.

Peter tells Christian wives to act like the godly wives of the Old Testament who trusted in God and submitted to their husbands. These women set the standard for the kind of attitude that Christian women are to have. Peter singles out Sarah, Abraham's wife, as an example of godly submission. She "obeyed" her husband and called him "lord," which was a term of respect and honor in her day.

It is important to note that Peter doesn't view Sarah's submission as part of the curse on women (Gen. 3:16). Rather, he views it as a model that receives divine approval. Sarah exercised her marital role as God intended.

3. Peter instructs Christian husbands to understand and honor their wives.

In 1 Peter 3:7, Peter has an equally important message for Christian husbands. Although the husband has a unique, leadership-authority role in the marriage relationship, he is to exercise his authority in a distinctly loving and Christian way.

a. Be an understanding husband

The first thing Peter says is to be an "understanding" husband. The word "understanding" is a good rendering of the Greek. Literally Peter writes, "living together according to knowledge." Thus living with a woman is "something a man must *know how* to do."[55] A Christian husband should also seek to be a learner and student of his wife. He should pursue insight, self-control, love, patience, grace, and wisdom in order to be an understanding husband.

Husbands and wives live together and share together the most intimate matters of human life—sexual, emotional, financial, and spiritual. To live successfully in such close, intimate relationship requires a great deal of effort and wisdom. It demands knowledge of God's design for the marriage relationship, especially God's teaching on headship and submission.

Some men, however, don't seem to have a clue about how to treat a woman. They are insensitive to their wife's needs and feelings. They can't understand their wife's frustrations and hurts. They are deceived about themselves. They think only of their own careers and self-fulfillment. They exhibit incredible selfishness and callousness. They are capable only of making women suffer. These men need to repent, seek counsel, and study God's word on Christian husbanding. First Peter 3 would be a good place for them to start.

b. Show honor to your wife

A Christian husband is to show special honor to his wife. Peter says, "grant [or show] her honor." Too many husbands make their wife feel worthless and unappreciated. They take her for granted; they intimidate, humiliate, criticize, and put down their wife. Some men seek to control their wife as if she is a little child, while others neglect their wife. This is not the behavior of a Christian husband; it is pagan behavior.

A Christian husband gladly honors his wife. He knows that she truly deserves a special place of honor. So he speaks well of her and to her. He tells her she is loved and needed and that he is blessed to be her husband. He prizes her counsel and seeks her correction. He reminds her that she is an indispensable part of his life, a special gift from the Lord, and has a worth that is "far above jewels" (Prov. 31:10).

Peter supplies three reasons for honoring and understanding one's wife.

(1) Weaker vessel. Peter first reminds the husband that the wife is the weaker vessel. Peter is not belittling women by calling them "the weaker vessel."

The husband is also a vessel. By *vessel* he means human being.

Peter also refers to her, not as "the wife," but as "the woman," "the female," "the feminine one." This reminds the husband of his wife's feminine nature. She is not a man. God created her with unique differences. The husband must understand the differences if he intends to live with his wife in an understanding way and properly honor her.

The wife is to be treated with special honor precisely because of her position as the more vulnerable partner. She is more vulnerable to physical, sexual, and emotional abuse, unjust treatment, and abandonment. That is why most cities have shelters to protect women from domestic violence, which is a growing worldwide problem. The husband, on the other hand, is physically stronger, more aggressive, and emotionally less sensitive. So the Christian husband must consider his wife's vulnerable position and not take unfair advantage of her.

Peter's remarks do not deny women's unique strengths and abilities (Prov. 31:10-31). Here he is reminding men of the woman's feminine nature in order to encourage them to be more understanding and honoring of their wives.

(2) Equals in spiritual life. Peter reminds the husband that his wife is "a fellow heir of the grace of life." The wife is the weaker vessel in terms of the marriage relationship on earth, but she is not weaker in spiritual life and destiny. The wife is a co-heir with her husband in salvation and eternal life (1:3-9), thus she is his equal in the faith. All Christian women as well as men belong to the "royal priesthood," "holy nation," and "people for God's own possession" (2:9).

(3) Divine discipline. Peter warns husbands that if they don't honor their wives, their prayers will be hindered. No man can afford to have his prayers hindered by God (v. 12). Such action by God means divine discipline.

God is serious about a man honoring his wife. A Christian husband cannot treat his wife harshly or neglect her and also be a spiritual man. God will not respond to a hypocritical husband who prays eloquently in front of the church, but treats his wife cruelly at home.

In summary, the Christian wife is to submit to her husband and the Christian husband is to be considerate of his wife and show her special honor. These are the teachings of our Lord as written by the apostle Peter.

B. Ephesians 5:21-33: Submission, Loving Headship, and a One-Flesh Union

Paul was not one of the twelve apostles, but he was an apostle. While Paul was still in his mother's womb, God set him aside for his special task of preaching and teaching Christ to the nations (Gal. 1:15, 16). On the now-famous road to Damascus, the risen, glorified Christ appeared and dramatically appointed Paul to be an apostle.

Like the Twelve, Paul is an official emissary of Christ; he can issue commands and require obedience. Therefore, Paul's instructions to Christian women and men are Christ's instructions. In the context of addressing the woman's role in a church meeting, Paul can say, "If anyone thinks he is a prophet or spiritual, let him recognize that the things which I write to you *are the Lord's commandment"* (1 Cor. 14:37; italics added).

Like Peter, Paul doesn't support sexism or woman hating when he defines the relationship of men and women in terms of headship and submission. Both of these men are Christ-appointed messengers who teach God's design for the sexes. To say that they were woman haters is to say that Christ was too.

Paul was not, as some say, a frustrated, old, male chauvinist rabbi who feared women. To paint Paul as a small-minded, hateful man grotesquely misrepresents the historical facts. The New Testament record reveals Paul to be a man of giant intellect and broad cultural experience. Yet it also portrays him as a man who was compassionate, completely self-sacrificing, humble, highly sensitive to the feelings of others, and—above all—loving. Love characterizes Paul's attitude toward women, and this attitude was formed by Christ's attitude toward women. That is why he can say with confidence to his converts, "Be imitators of me, just as I also am of Christ" (1 Cor. 11:1).

Paul, the same man who instructed women to submit to their husbands, penned the greatest words ever written on love: "If I speak with the tongues of men and of angels, but do not have love, I have become a noisy gong or a clanging cymbal. If I have the gift of prophecy, and know all mysteries and all knowledge; and if I have all faith, so as to remove mountains, but do not have love, I am nothing" (1 Cor. 13:1, 2). Furthermore, a woman hater doesn't tell a husband to love his wife with a Christlike self-sacrificing love or to be ready to die for her, as Paul does in Ephesians 5 (see also 1 Cor. 7:4, 5).

Let us now briefly survey five of Paul's passages on marriage (Eph. 5:21-33; Col. 3:18,19; 1 Cor. 7; Titus 2:4, 5; 1 Tim. 3:4, 5), starting with Ephesians 5, which stands out among the lofty biblical passages on Christian marriage. It may well be the most profound passage of our study addressing the gender issue. The study of Ephesians 5 should be a part of any Christian premarital counseling program and marriage ceremony.

This towering passage defines the basic structure of Christian marriage: a one-flesh union between a man and a woman that is characterized by the wife's willing submission to her husband and the husband's loving leadership and care for his wife. The perfect model for this marital union is the oneness of the Christ-Church relationship, with Christ as the loving Head of the relationship and the Church being submissive to Him in everything.

God therefore defines marriage as a union in which distinct roles are prescribed for each partner. To deny these differences in marriage is to deny marriage as God designed it. More than any other passage in Scripture, Ephesians 5 makes this point crystal clear.

Moreover, according to Ephesians 5, the key to the headship-submission relationship is love. Without love, this doctrine readily deteriorates into male chauvinism. That is why it is absolutely essential that the full teaching of the complete passage be made clear.

The first step in accurate Bible study and interpretation begins with careful and repeated reading of the text itself. Take some time to methodically and thoughtfully read the verses below.

5:21 and be subject to one another in the fear of Christ.

5:22 Wives, be subject to your own husbands, as to the Lord.

5:23 For the husband is the head of the wife, as Christ also is the head of the church, He Himself being the Savior of the body.

5:24 But as the church is subject to Christ, so also the wives ought to be to their husbands in everything.

5:25 Husbands, love your wives, just as Christ also loved the church and gave Himself up for her;

5:26 so that He might sanctify her, having cleansed her by the washing of water with the word,

5:27 that He might present to Himself the church in all her glory, having no spot or wrinkle or any such thing; but that she should be holy and blameless.

1. Paul instructs wives to submit to their husbands.

In clear, straightforward style, Paul instructs Christian wives to submit to their husbands: "Wives, be subject to your own husbands, as to the Lord" (v. 22). The Greek verb for "be subject to" *(hypotassō)* is the same verb used in 1 Peter 3:1. It "means to take a subordinate role in relation to that of another."[56]

Commenting on the wife's submission in Ephesians 5 and Colossians 3, George Knight III, biblical commentator and former New Testament professor at Knox Theological Seminary, observes: "This particular exhortation to the wife to submit to her husband is the universal teaching of the New Testament. Every passage that deals with the relationship of the wife to her husband tells her to 'submit to' him, using this same verb *(hypotassō):* Ephesians 5:22; Colossians 3:18; 1 Peter 3:1; Titus 2:4ff."[57]

Some commentators insist that Ephesians 5 teaches "mutual submission" between husband and wife. They cite Ephesians 5:21, "and be subject *[hypotassō]* to one another in the fear of Christ," and conclude that the husband should submit to the wife in the same way that the wife should submit to the husband. This interpretation of Ephesians 5:21 is mistaken, however. One cannot use verse 21 to sweep away the plain teaching of verses 22-23. There is no conflict between verse 21 and verses 22-23. What is meant by "be subject to one another" is explained in specific detail in the verses that follow. The specifics include wives being subject to their husbands.

Of course, there is a sense in which the husband as a godly leader defers to his wife's wise counsel, correction, or requests. True love submits—even sacrifices—itself for the benefit of another (see 1 Cor. 7:3-5). But the sacrifices of Christlike love do not eliminate the headship-submission structure of the marriage. The husband still retains an authority the wife does not have, an authority to which a godly wife willingly submits.

Ephesians 5:21 and Mutual Submission

First, the verb "subject to," as already explained in comments on 1 Peter 3:1, always indicates one-directional submission to an authority, not mutual submission.

Second, the Greek pronoun for "one another" can mean either "everyone to everyone" (something that every single person does to every single other person) or "some to others." In this case, the full context and the verb "be subject to" require the rendering "some to others," meaning the wife to the husband.

The context (5:22 to 6:9) specifies three special groups about which Paul is concerned. Thus he lists for us the appropriate authorities to whom submission is due within each group—wives to husbands (5:22), children to parents (6:1), and slaves to masters (6:5). Thus verse 21 does not hang in mid air; it is explained and expanded upon in the following verses (5:22 to 6:9). So the full context doesn't allow for the idea of equal submission between the marriage partners, any more than it teaches that parents should submit to children and masters should obey their servants.

Third, if Paul had intended to teach Christian couples in the male-dominated culture of the first century that the husband was to submit to his wife in the same way that she submitted to him, he utterly failed to make his point. Indeed, he did a superb job of making the opposite point. Using grandiose theological images, Paul explicitly teaches that the wife is to submit to her husband as the Church submits to Christ and the husband is the head of the wife as Christ is head of the Church. This certainly would be a strange way to teach mutual submission if that was his intent. Surely the first-century Christian husband needed to hear in unequivocal language that he was to submit to his wife in a relationship of mutual submission, but he would not have heard such teaching from Ephesians 5:23-33.

a. Submit as to the Lord

The Christian wife is to submit to her husband "as to the Lord," meaning as to Jesus Christ. George Knight comments: "The comparative 'as to the Lord' conjures up what should and does characterize the godly submission a Christian renders to the Lord Jesus. This one qualification says it all."[58] This little phrase tells us that the wife's submission to her husband is a part of her submission to the Lord Jesus Christ. So Jesus endorses the principle of the wife's submission and would have her submit to her husband as unto Him.

b. A profound theological reason for submission

Ephesians 5 is immensely important to our topic because it explains why the wife should submit. After exhorting wives to submit to their husbands (v. 22), Paul immediately provides the reason: "For the husband is the head of the wife, as Christ also is the head of the church" (v. 23). Note the following two points.

(1) The husband is the head. Scripture doesn't say the husband *should* be the head of the wife, but *is* the head of the wife. Neuer's excellent comment deserves repeating:

> Just as one cannot confess Jesus Christ without affirming his lordship, so it is impossible to confess maleness without affirming male headship. When men refuse to accept their particular responsibility to be head of the wife, they are rebelling against the position intended by God and living in contradiction to their nature as males. God has put the husband over his wife in a similar way to that in which he put Christ over the church.[59]

This particular exhortation to the wife to submit to her husband is the universal teaching of the New Testament. Every passage that deals with the relationship of the wife to her husband tells her to "submit to" him, using this same verb *(hypotassō)*. GEORGE KNIGHT

---

(2) The husband's headship is based on Christ's headship. The basis for the husband's headship is not first-century Roman culture; rather it is Christ and His Church. Here is the most compelling argument that headship in Christian marriage is not cultural but is divinely planned: The husband is the head of the wife as Christ is the head of the Church. Christ and His redeemed people, the Church, are the ground and motivation for wifely submission and male leadership. The perfect model for human marriage is the relationship between Christ and His Church.

The word "head" is another of the four key terms driving the gender debate. To advance in the debate you must grasp the correct meaning of this word.

The Greek word for "head" is *kephalē*. This is the common Greek word for the literal, physical head on the human body, but it is also used in the figurative (metaphorical) sense of "one in a position of authority" or "leader." Since the literal head is at the top of the body and directs the body, *head* readily becomes a metaphor for a leader or authority figure. We use the figurative (metaphorical) sense of head when we say that one is "the head of state" or "the head of a department in a university or business."

Christ is said to be "head over all things." Ephesians 1:22 tells us that "[God] put all things in subjection under [Christ's] feet, and gave Him as head over all things to the church." So, when Paul makes the direct, clear, statement in Ephesians 5:23 that the husband is the head of the wife, he means that the husband is the leader, the authority figure in the marriage relationship. As leader, he gives direction to the family and is ultimately responsible to provide for its well being. The wife should submit to her husband because the husband is the God-appointed "head."

Scripture doesn't say the husband *should* be the head of the wife, but *is* the head of the wife.

Feminist interpreters fiercely protest this conclusion. They refuse to accept that the word "head" means "one in authority." They claim that the word "head" in Ephesians 5:23 means "origin" or "life source" without the meaning of authority. They believe the husband is the source of the wife in the sense of life-giving love, service, and help to the wife. In the words of Rebecca Groothuis, the wife is thus to "submit to life."[60]

Wayne Grudem, who understands the critical importance of rightly translating the word "head,"[61] makes this claim: "I once looked up over 2,300 examples of the word 'head' *(kephalē)* in ancient Greek. In these texts, the word *kephale* is applied to many people in authority, but to none without governing authority."[62] He concludes, *"In the Greek-speaking world, to be the head of a group of people always meant to have authority over those people"*[63]

Grudem goes on to say that if someone claims that the word *head* means "source" or "origin" without the sense of authority, to ask that person the following question: *"You claim that the Greek word for 'head' means 'source without the idea of authority.' Will you please show me one example in all of ancient Greek where this word (kephalē) is used to refer to a person and means what you claim, namely, 'non-authoritative source'?"*[64] Grudem concludes:

> Wherever one person is said to be the "head" of another person (or persons), the person who is called the "head" is always the one in authority (such as the general of an army, the Roman emperor, Christ, the heads of the tribes of Israel, David as head of the nations, etc.) Specifically, we cannot find any text [in Greek literature] where person A is called the "head" of person or persons B, and is not in a position of authority over that person or persons.[65]

Furthermore, the entire context of Ephesians 5:21-6:9 regarding submission and leadership in the relationships of wife and husband, child and parent, and slave and master should alone solve the issue of the meaning of the term "head."

**Here is the most compelling argument
that headship in Christian marriage is not cultural
but is divinely planned: The husband is the head of
the wife as Christ is the head of the Church.**

In verse 22, the wife is instructed to submit to her husband who is called "the head of the wife." This can only mean that the husband is an authority figure (head). Otherwise, the instruction to submit is meaningless. As one scholar rightly concludes, "only with violence to the text can it be asserted that the idea of authority is absent from the language of headship and submission in Ephesians 5:22-33."[66]

Key word: *Head* (Greek, *kephalē*)

The word *head (kephalē)* is used in the figurative sense of "one in authority over," or "leader." When the Scripture says, "the husband is the head of the wife," it means he is the leader of the two people, the authority figure. The word "head" *does not* mean "source of" or "origin."

---

c. The wife's submission is based on the Church's submission

The basis for the wife's submission is not first-century Roman culture, it is Christ and His Church. Paul says that the wife is to subject herself to her husband "as the church is subject to Christ" (v. 24). In Christian marriage, the wife represents the Church that freely and willingly submits to Christ's headship, and the husband represents Christ, the self-giving, loving head of the Church.

2. Paul instructs husbands to love their wives as Christ loved the Church.

Up to this point in Ephesians 5, we have focused on Paul's instruction regarding wives' submission to their husbands (Eph. 5:22-24). Now we turn our attention to Paul's instruction to husbands to love their wives (Eph. 5:25-32). Ephesians 5 teaches profound and amazing truths, but one of the most revolutionary concepts is that Christian husbands are to love their wives as Christ loved the Church. David Martyn Lloyd-Jones expresses masterfully the ground-breaking nature of this command:

> This statement, when it was written by the Apostle, was one of the most astounding that had ever been put on paper. When we read of the pagan view of marriage, and especially the typical attitude of husbands toward wives—and, indeed, not only pagan, but also what you read of in the Old Testament—we see how revolutionary and transforming the teaching is.[67]

Tragically, some Christian men think that headship means dictatorship or lordship—being the boss. Thus the Christian doctrine of headship has been misused to justify the physical and mental abuse of women, keeping women "in their place," demeaning and controlling women, working wives to death, or neglecting them. But Christian husbands who abuse or neglect their wives don't understand authentic Christian marriage. They don't understand loving, servant leadership, and they certainly don't understand Ephesians 5.

The standard for regulating the husband's leadership is Christ's own self-sacrificing love.

Ephesians 5 does not command the husband to rule or take control of his wife. Nor does it tell husbands to force their wives to be subject. Rather, it commands the husband to love as Christ loves. In the wise words of one theologian: "The vocation of the husband's 'headship' does not imply that the man's will ought necessarily to prevail. Paul does not speak of the husband having his way, but of his love sacrifice."[68] Prolific author and pastor John Piper gives us the right perspective when he says, "The husband who plops himself in front of the TV and orders his wife around like a slave has abandoned Christ for Archie Bunker."[69]

Another misuse of this passage that needs correction is the practice of preaching to wives about submission while neglecting to teach the husbands' duty to love their wives as Christ loves the Church. Many male chauvinists have the ability to ignore the Ephesians 5 command that a husband love his wife and to focus exclusively on the woman's submission. They seem to think the only thing the Bible says about marriage is "wives submit." This is a striking imbalance because most of Ephesians 5 addresses the husband's duty to love his wife (vv. 25-32). The greater responsibility falls on the husband to imitate Christ's loving leadership.

Mary Kassian, a leading author and spokeswoman for the complementarian position, expresses pointedly the frustration many women feel regarding this unfairness:

> Teaching on marital roles has often been lopsided. Many preach on woman's submission without allotting equal time to man's corresponding responsibilities. This is a source of endless frustration to women. They constantly hear how they are to submit, yet they seldom hear that this is tempered by the husband's responsibility to love.
>
> As a result, some women have rebelled against biblical teaching. As well, the overemphasis on the woman's role has led men to believe that it is their duty as spiritual leaders to help their wives learn submission. This belief fosters a harsh, domineering, and chauvinistic attitude that makes it even more difficult for women to fulfill their role. Much bitterness and rebellion could be avoided if the emphasis on marital roles were correctly placed on the male role of loving leadership rather than on the female role of submission.[70]

a. Loving one's wife as Christ loves the Church

The standard for regulating the husband's leadership is Christ's own self-sacrificing love. Christ loved the Church, and He demonstrated His love in the deepest way possible. He gave *Himself* for His bride. He died for her (v. 25). He is "the Savior of the body" (v. 23). "More excellent love than that is inconceivable."[71] Christ also sanctifies and cleanses her (v. 26), and He will see to her full glorification in the future (v. 27). Christ will present His bride (the Church) to Himself, holy and blameless, as He, the bridegroom, is holy and blameless (v. 27). This is the kind of costly, comprehensive, loving headship that Christ exercises over His Church. This is *agape* love, selfless, self-giving love.

Likewise, Christian husbands are, in this highest sense, to love their wives. They are to give their all for their wives—even their lives if necessary (v. 25). They are to protect their wives from evil influences and cultivate their spiritual perfection and beauty. "The Lord's pattern of love for His church is the husband's pattern of love for his wife."[72] As a result, the distinguishing mark of the Christian home should be selfless, self-sacrificing love initiated by the husband. This is the kind of leadership husbands should provide for their wives.

The Christian home and church, above all other institutions, should be the places where women are loved and honored, not neglected and used.

Ephesians 5 certainly cuts the chains of male exploitation of women. The Christian home and church, above all other institutions, should be the places where women are loved and honored, not neglected and used. Men, take heed to these powerful, challenging words!

b. Loving one's wife as one's own body

Verses 28 to 33 form a new section. Here, Paul restates that husbands ought to love their wives. He then adds a profound new reason for this love: the unique oneness of the husband-wife relationship. The husband and wife are not two, but one flesh, one person. This entire section is governed by the Genesis 2:24 statement quoted in verse 31: "the two shall become one flesh." Ephesians 5:28-33:

> **5:28** So husbands ought also to love their own wives as their own bodies. He who loves his own wife loves himself;
>
> **5:29** for no one ever hated his own flesh, but nourishes and cherishes it, just as Christ also does the church,
>
> **5:30** because we are members of His body.
>
> **5:31** for this reason a man shall leave his father and mother and shall be joined to his wife, and the two shall become one flesh.
>
> **5:32** This mystery is great; but I am speaking with reference to Christ and the church.
>
> **5:33** Nevertheless, each individual among you also is to love his own wife even as himself, and the wife must see to it that she respects her husband.

(1) Husband and wife are one body, one flesh, one person. Verse 28 exhorts husbands "to love their own wives as their own bodies." The essential thing about marriage is unity, oneness, and togetherness. The marriage bond creates an intimate, permanent, "one flesh" union between a man and a woman. The husband and wife are not two isolated individuals, they are one. "In the light of this," Lloyd-Jones insightfully writes, "the husband must no longer think singly or individually."[73] The husband ought to love his wife sacrificially because she is a part of himself.

Logically, then, the husband should act toward his wife as he acts toward his own body for which he naturally cares. All normal people love their bodies in the sense that they care for the body's many practical needs, such as food, clothing, and shelter. So Christian husbands are to affectionately nourish and cherish their wives and tenderly care for their many practical needs, just as they care for their own body's needs and comforts (vv. 28, 29). Furthermore, the oneness of the husband-wife relationship is so real that for a man to neglect or harm his wife is to neglect or harm himself.

One of the chief goals of marriage as it is presented in Scripture is unity and oneness. What is essential to understand is that *unity* in marriage is intimately connected to headship and submission. To achieve the reality of this one-flesh relationship, the husband is to selflessly lead and care for his wife in the way that Christ leads and cares for the Church, and the wife is to submit to and support her husband's leadership in the same way that the Church submits to and supports Christ's leadership. Although husband and wife have different roles in the marriage relationship, they both promote the interests, fulfillment, and well-being of the other.

(2) Christ and His people are one Body. After charging husbands to love their wives as their own bodies, Paul returns to the comparison of Christ and the Church (vv. 29-32): "for no one ever hated his own flesh, but nourishes and cherishes it [his body], just as Christ also does the church, because we are members of His body." Again, Christ's care for the Church (v. 29) is the perfect model presented for the husband to imitate.

Verse 30 reminds all believers that they comprise "His body," and because they are members of "His body," Christ can do nothing other than to nourish and cherish each and every member. He loves His Body, and He goes to great lengths to care for it. In the marriage relationship, the husband is to follow Christ's example.

(3) A great mystery. Immediately following the mention of "His body," Paul quotes Genesis 2:24, the Old Testament marriage passage that is first applied to Adam and Eve: "for this reason a man shall leave his father and mother and shall be joined to his wife, and the two shall become one flesh." The marriage union, unlike any other relationship on earth, uniquely makes two people into one person, one body, one flesh. Why does Paul quote this Old Testament text on marriage and apply it to Christ and His Body? He does

so because the relationship between Christ and His Body is an unbreakable, permanent, loving union like marriage is.

After applying Genesis 2:24 to Christ and His Body, Paul declares: "This mystery is great; but I am speaking with reference to Christ and the church" (Eph. 5:32). The word "mystery" means "a revealed secret," a divine plan or purpose that was previously hidden and inaccessible but is now revealed by God in Christ and proclaimed to all who will believe. "In the ordinary sense a mystery implies knowledge withheld; its Scriptural significance is truth revealed."[74]

The true marriage is that between Christ and His Church. All other marriages, including that in the Garden, are faint images...of the Marriage of the Lamb with His Bride, the Church.   WILLIAM WEINRICH

"This mystery" that is so wonderful or great refers to the hidden, prophetic meaning of Genesis 2:24. The concealed truth here revealed is that Genesis 2:24, the one-flesh relationship between Adam and Eve, is a prophetic image of the union between the risen Christ and His redeemed people. So the true fulfillment of Genesis 2:24 is found in the relationship of Christ and His Church. "The true marriage is that between Christ and His Church. All other marriages, including that in the Garden, are faint images...of the Marriage of the Lamb with His Bride, the Church."[75] The standard, then, for marriage is Christ and His Church, not male domination or egalitarian marriage. Thus we conclude that the headship-submission relationship in marriage is not an evil to be stamped out of existence. On the contrary, it is God's beautiful design for marriage. "It is part of the essence of marriage."[76]

The Ephesians 5 passage concludes in verse 33 with exhortations to the husband "to love his own wife even as himself and for the wife to "see to it that she respects her husband." The Greek word for "respect" is *phobos,* which can range in meaning from terror or fear to respect or reverence. In this context, "respect" is an acceptable English rendering. The wife respects her husband in the sense that she recognizes that he is her God-appointed head, her husband. As one commentator remarks, *"phobos* is a normal element in all authority structures."[77] Because the husband is her head in the marriage relationship, the wife not only needs to submit to him, she also needs to "respect her husband."

C. Colossians 3:18, 19: Submission and Love

Here Paul presents to the church at Colossae a shortened version of Ephesians 5. Even in its abbreviated form, it is still the Word of God and merits our full attention. Paul says,

> **3:18** Wives, be subject to your husbands, as is fitting in the Lord.
> **3:19** Husbands, love your wives, and do not be embittered against them.

Again, Paul directly instructs Christian wives to "be subject" (Greek, *hypotassō)* to their husbands. If wives are to submit to their husbands, then we may assume that husbands must be the leaders of the relationship. Note that nothing is said here about mutual submission between husband and wife.

Paul follows the exhortation with an extremely important reason and motivation for submission: "as is fitting in the Lord." The word "fitting" means "the right thing to do," "what is proper, one's duty."[78] Submitting to one's husband, then, is the right thing to do.

The phrase "in the Lord" specifies that submission is the proper behavior under the lordship of Jesus Christ and in the community of people who profess Jesus as Lord. The wife's submission then represents proper Christian behavior, what the Lord Jesus requires, and what the Christian community expects. Submission is not based on the husband's merits; it is based on the will of Jesus our Lord.

The husband also has his duty to perform in the marriage. Paul writes: "Husbands, love your wives, and do not be embittered against them." As in Ephesians 5, the husband is commanded to *love* his wife—not to rule her, boss her, control her, break her, or enslave her. The *love* that is Christian love is defined by God. Commentator Peter O'Brien describes the nature of this love: "This is not simply a matter of affectionate feeling or sexual attraction; rather, it involves his unceasing care and loving service for her entire well-being....It is a love that is sacrificial, that disregards itself, which is defined by Christ's action."[79]

A special warning follows: husbands "do not be embittered against them [wives]." Here is a specific example of a lack of love, which is a common male problem. In the daily pressures of life, husbands are inclined to take out their frustrations on their wives; to speak with harsh words and to cast disapproving looks; to be sour, cross, crabby, impatient, or irritable; and to criticize and find fault. "In a strange quirk of human behavior we can often injure thoughtlessly those we love the most."[80] Such behavior, however, is contrary to our Lord's will. He warns against it and prohibits it.

D. 1 Corinthians 7:1-40: Divorce, Singleness, and Marital Obligations

First Corinthians deals with many practical issues and problems that affect all local churches throughout all times. No one can ever criticize 1 Corinthians for being boring or too theoretical: every chapter pulsates with real-life situations confronting the newly planted church in the worldly city of Corinth. So it is not surprising that Paul addresses male-female relationship issues four times in the letter (6:12-20, 7:1-40, 11:2-16, 14:34-37). These topics spark white-hot debate today, just as they did in Paul's time.

The Corinthians wrote Paul to ask for clarification on issues he had addressed in a letter written to them previously (1 Cor. 7:1, 5:9). One question was about marriage. Distorted views about sex, marriage, and divorce plagued the church, so, in chapter 7, Paul confronts those issues and questions.

When giving directives regarding divorce, Paul treats husbands and wives equally. The same holds true for his counsel on singleness (7:7-9, 25-35). He encourages single women as well as single men to use their status as an opportunity to serve the Lord with undivided devotion (7:32-35). Not all women need to marry and have children. Like men, women can use their singleness to serve God fully.

What is particularly relevant to our study is Paul's unique emphasis on the full, reciprocal, sexual rights and duties of husbands and wives within marriage. No mention of headship or submission appears here. Feminists and complementarians happily find much agreement in this chapter.

Read these verses selected from the seventh chapter of 1 Corinthians:

> **7:3** The husband must fulfill his duty to his wife, and likewise also the wife to her husband.
>
> **7:4** The wife does not have authority over her own body, but the husband does; and likewise also the husband does not have authority over his own body, but the wife does.
>
> **7:5** Stop depriving one another, except by agreement for a time, so that you may devote yourselves to prayer, and come together again so that Satan will not tempt you because of your lack of self-control.

Some Christians in Corinth were advocating sexual abstinence within marriage. Paul emphatically forbids such a practice: "Stop depriving one another" (v. 5). Sexual relations within marriage are not an option; they are a duty, an obligation: "The husband must fulfill his duty [sexually] to his wife, and likewise also the wife to her husband" (v. 3). To refuse one's spouse is to deprive (or "defraud") that spouse of what rightfully belongs to him or her—sexual fulfillment and the partner's body.

Paul does, however, allow for sexual abstinence within marriage under temporary, *mutually agreed upon* occasions: "Stop depriving one another [sexually], except *by agreement* for a time, so that you may devote yourselves to prayer, and come together again [sexually] so that Satan will not tempt you because of your lack of self-control" (v. 5; italics added).

In verse 4, Paul makes one of the most amazing statements about marriage in the whole Bible: "The wife does not have authority over her own body, but the husband does; and likewise also the husband does not have authority over his own body, but the wife does" (v. 4). This is a powerful declaration of equality between the sexes and oneness in marriage. "It is the exact parallelism, that is most striking here. Conjugal rights are equal and reciprocal."[81]

The husband's leadership (headship) in the marriage, then, must take into account the principle of mutual sexual obligations and pleasures. Sex is not the man's prerogative. The wife's needs and pleasure must be considered equally.

The wife does not have authority over her own body, but the husband does; and likewise also the husband does not have authority over his own body, but the wife does. PAUL

The husband does not have complete authority over his body to do as he pleases. The wife has *God-given authority* over her husband's body, and he over her body. "Neither husband nor wife is given more rights over the body of the other."[82] In the language of lovers, the beautiful love song of The Song of Solomon expresses it best: "My beloved is mine, and I am his" (2:16).

E. Titus 2:3-5: Teaching Younger Wives Love and Submission.

Writing to his colleague Titus and through him to the churches on the Island of Crete, Paul instructs older, mature wives to encourage younger wives to love their husbands and children; to be sensible, kind, and pure; to be home-makers; and to be submissive to their husbands.

For Christian wives and mothers, Titus 2:4, 5 is profoundly significant. It teaches that their primary responsibilities center on their husbands, children, and homes. Robert Lewis and William Hendricks, in their excellent book *Rocking the Roles: Building a Win-Win Marriage,* write:

> I believe this list of responsibilities in Titus 2:4-5 represents the most succinct summary of a woman's core role in all of Scripture. This defines the term *helper* (the title given by God to Eve in Genesis 2:18) in clear and specific terms....
>
> ...A core role is not everything a woman does in marriage. She is not confined only to what Paul describes here. But she dare not excuse herself from these responsibilities or neglect them for other ambitions. Like the planets around the sun, everything in marriage should revolve around these crucial core-role responsibilities and concerns. A wife's core role should prioritize her commitments and her use of energy and time. It should keep her from missing out on what God has called her to do in her life and in her marriage.
>
> It also should give stability to her marriage, because it provides a grid through which she can filter, measure, and evaluate all the opportunities that come her way. Unfortunately, the mistake many women are making today is in treating these core-role responsibilities as just options in a myriad of options. But a core role is not an opinion. It's a biblical absolute.[83]

In a culture that is obsessed with self-fulfillment and the idea that marriage adversely affects a woman's health and career, Titus 2 needs to be clearly heard and affirmed by Christian couples:

> **2:3** Older women likewise are to be reverent in their behavior, not malicious gossips nor enslaved to much wine, teaching what is good,
>
> **2:4** so that they may encourage the young women to love their husbands, to love their children,
>
> **2:5** to be sensible, pure, workers at home, kind, being subject to their own husbands, so that the word of God will not be dishonored.

Titus 2 begins with a strong warning to Titus to "speak the things which are fitting for sound doctrine" (2:1). By the terms "sound doctrine" Paul means sound Christian teaching. What is stated here about wives and mothers is sound Christian doctrine, not Greco-Roman law. Sound Christian doctrine charges older, mature wives to teach and model Christian womanhood for younger wives. Paul lists seven specific virtues that mature Christian wives are to teach younger wives. We will focus on four of these.

1. Love your husband.

A wife's core role is to help her husband (Gen. 2:18), and loving him is essential to that role. In a sinful world, it is not easy for a woman to live with a man. To love is difficult, and many men don't make it any easier. The mounting pressures and conflicts of marriage can squelch the fire of a woman's love for her husband, so she needs to be encouraged to love, especially when it is not easy.

Marriage provides the best school in which to learn self-sacrificing, Christlike love. An older Christian woman can be a great teacher and adviser to a younger wife in the school of marital love. Loving one's spouse is the first and foremost course of study. When a wife loves her husband, all else in the marriage fits into place more easily.

2. Love your children.

For a Christian mother, another core responsibility is to care for her children. Children are to be a priority in her life. In many developed countries of the world today, an anti-birth, anti-child mentality permeates society. Bible-believing Christians, however, must affirm the paramount value of children and motherhood. Dorothy Patterson, one of the authors of *Recovering Biblical Manhood and Womanhood,* puts the issue into focus: "A mother builds something far more magnificent than any cathedral—the dwelling place for an immortal soul.... No professional pursuit so uniquely combines the most menial tasks with the most meaningful opportunities."[84]

Mothers need to be encouraged and counseled to love their children, give them full attention, value them above material possessions and personal career, and teach them God's Holy Word for salvation (2 Tim. 1:5, 3:15). Patterson expresses best the need of the hour: "There is no greater need for the coming years than a revival of interest in the responsibilities of motherhood."[85] Older, experienced mothers have a God-given mandate to encourage younger mothers to love their children.

> **A core role is not everything a woman does in marriage. She is not confined only to what Paul describes here.... A wife's core role should prioritize her commitments and her use of energy and time.** LEWIS AND HENDRICKS

3. Be a diligent homemaker.

Another core responsibility for a wife and mother is the management of the home. In the words of Proverbs 31:27: "She looks well to the ways of her household." Older, experienced wives are to encourage younger wives to be diligent homemakers. The home can be the most pleasant place on earth, and wives have the special privilege of being managers of the home. They care for its daily needs, beauty, creativity, and comfort. It is a career that is indispensable to the health and education of the whole human race.

4. Be submissive to your husband.

In line with the wife's role of helper is the response of submission. This, too, must be taught and encouraged. Older, experienced wives are to encourage younger wives to be submissive (Greek, *hypotassō)* to their husbands. Even in a Christian home headed by a godly husband, submission can be trying to the soul. It is at times perplexing to implement. So younger wives need wise counsel and help from experienced sisters in the Lord. Furthermore, young Christian wives need to be encouraged to prize their roles as helper, wife, mother, and homemaker, not just to tolerate them or to treat them as another curious religious theory. Even submission to one's husband can be prized when it is understood as the Creator's will and design for the wife.

Paul concludes by reminding both older and younger women that their non-Christian neighbors and relatives regularly observe their behavior. So, Scripture says, live in such a way "that the word of God may not be dishonored." Mary Kassian summarizes the point well: "Women who neglect their homes, their family, or their marriage discredit Christ."[86]

F. 1 Timothy 3:4, 5, 12: Men as Good Family Leaders

A biblical qualification for both church overseers and deacons is the ability to manage one's family well (especially the children, v. 4), which means that a church leader's family must be above reproach. Paul underscores the importance of this requirement with a rhetorical question: "But if a man does not know how to manage his own household, how will he take care of the church of God?" The answer to that question is a resounding negative: he can't care for the church of God if he doesn't know how to manage his own family.

> **3:2** An overseer, then, must be above reproach, the husband of one wife....
>
> **3:4** He must be one who manages his own household well, keeping his children under control with all dignity
>
> **3:5** (but if a man does not know how to manage his own household, how will he take care of the church of God?).

According to Scripture, an overseer's life should provide the local church family with a living model of Christian behavior that others should follow (1 Peter 5:3). Since an overseer (elder) must manage his family well, all Christian men should follow that model and strive to be good family leaders.

We see from the preceding Scripture texts (Titus 2:4, 5; 1 Tim. 3:4, 5) that Christian husbands and wives, under the husband's headship, work as a team. They support each other, and they depend upon each other.

Questions

1. Why do most contemporary people respond so negatively to the word *submission?* List two reasons.

2. What point does Professor Wayne Grudem making concerning the Greek word *(hypotassō)* for *submission?*

3. Does a wife have to submit to every demand her husband makes? Can you think of an example that supports your answer?

4. Why should a woman be more concerned about inner beauty than external beauty? List three reasons.

5. According to 1 Peter 3:7, how is a Christian husband to treat his wife? Can you think of some positive, marital examples to illustrate your answers?

6. How would you respond to someone who believes that Paul hated women? List some Scripture passages that support your answer.

7. What does the word *head* mean in Ephesians 5? How would you explain your answer?

8. In what ways does Ephesians 5 show that the headship-submission doctrine is not a cultural practice but a Christian doctrine?

9. In what ways do men misuse the Bible's teaching on marital headship (leadership)? List at least three ways.

10. Describe the unique kind of marital headship (leadership) Paul writes about in Ephesians 5. Cite one practical example of this kind of leadership in a marriage.

11. What does 1 Corinthians 7:3-5 teach Christian couples, particularly husbands, about their marital responsibilities?

12. According to Titus 2, what are the primary, core responsibilities of a wife and mother?

13. Why does a church overseer (pastor, elder) have to manage his family well in order to qualify for church leadership? List two reasons.

14. What did you learn from this chapter that will help shape your thinking and actions regarding headship and submission in the family?

IV. Through His Apostles, Jesus Christ Taught Gender Equality and Role Differences in the Christian Community

I have to admit it," Tom says, "the apostles' arguments for the headship submission relationship in marriage are powerful and convincing."

"That's good! There's a reason we started with Christian marriage before looking at men and women in the church family."

"What's that?" Tom asks.

"If you don't understand God's design for marriage and the family, you can't understand the New Testament's instructions for men and women in the church family."

"Why is that?" Tom asks.

"Many people don't understand the New Testament's view of men and women in the church because they don't understand the intimate relationship between the individual family and the extended family, which is the local church. Just as Paul teaches masculine leadership in the individual family, he teaches masculine leadership in the extended local church family. So an understanding of leadership in the family is essential to an understanding of leadership in the church family."

"That makes sense."

"Furthermore, in the minds of the New Testament writers, the Church is the household of God and gender distinctions are an important part of God's plan for His people. The local church is to model God's design for the sexes. So, headship and submission must be taught and practiced in the local church."

"I know already what my friends are going to say," Tom quickly responds. "I can hear it now: this is all cultural. Gender distinctions aren't all that important in our society. You're taking the Bible too literally."

"Tom, your friends simply aren't allowing the Scriptures to speak for themselves. They're playing fast and loose with the words of Scripture. Paul backs up what he says about men and women in the church family with the strongest possible arguments: the Genesis creation accounts, the universal practice of all the churches, the relationship of the members of the Trinity, a command of Christ, and his own apostolic authority. These are not cultural arguments."

"Okay, but don't equality between the sexes and masculine headship contradict each other? That is what I've been told," Tom responds.

"No, both truths represent the full truth of how God designed the sexes."

"Well, I'm ready to study the passages that address men and women in the church family," Tom says, "because that's where most of my questions arise."

Since the family is the fundamental social unit and the man is the established family leader, we should not be surprised that men would also be the leaders of the local church family. The local church family should be a model of masculine headship and women's submission from which individual families can learn how to follow God's design for the family. Stephen Clark cogently highlights this principle:

> There is a further consideration which points toward the desirability of having the men be the elders of the Christian community...the structure of leadership has to be set up in a way that supports the entire social structure of the [church] community. If the men are supposed to be the heads of the family, they must also be the heads of the community. The community must be structured in a way that supports the pattern of the family, and the family must be structured in a way that supports the pattern of the community. It is in the family that they learn their community roles as well. Conversely, what they see in the community reinforces what they learn in the family. Thus, to adopt different principles on the community level weakens the family, and vice versa.[87]

Let us now examine what the New Testament Scriptures teach about men and women in the church family.

A. 1 Timothy 2:8-15: Submission and Leadership in the Church Family

If Ephesians 5 is the crowning passage on Christian marriage, then 1 Timothy 2 is the crowning passage for gender roles in the local church family. First Timothy 2 is to the local church family what Ephesians 5 is to the individual family. First Timothy 2 is also the clearest and most prominent passage that restricts women from certain teaching and leadership ministries. So it is not surprising that, like Genesis 2, 1 Timothy 2 is a strategic battleground passage in the gender controversy.[88] Major critical assaults target this passage. Every word, phrase, and sentence has been disputed, yet no interpreter can avoid its looming presence and forceful declarations.

Because it is critical to grasp the meaning of this passage, please don't skip the first step in understanding the passage—direct exposure to the passage through careful, methodical reading. Pray for special discernment as you read and study 1 Timothy 2:8-15:

> **2:8** Therefore I want the men in every place to pray, lifting up holy hands, without wrath and dissension.
>
> **2:9** Likewise, I want women to adorn themselves with proper clothing, modestly and discreetly, not with braided hair and gold or pearls or costly garments,
>
> **2:10** but rather by means of good works, as is proper for women making a claim to godliness.
>
> **2:11** A woman must quietly receive instruction with entire submissiveness.
>
> **2:12** But I do not allow a woman to teach or exercise authority over a man, but to remain quiet.
>
> **2:13** For it was Adam who was first created, and then Eve.
>
> **2:14** And it was not Adam who was deceived, but the woman being deceived, fell into transgression.
>
> **2:15** But women will be preserved through the bearing of children if they continue in faith and love and sanctity with self-restraint.

It is important to note the circumstances under which this letter was written. After a brief and unpleasant visit to the church at Ephesus, Paul left Timothy there to stop the spread of false teaching and to restore the principles of church order to the church family. In this letter to Timothy, which was written shortly after Paul's departure from Ephesus, Paul deals with (among other items) proper treatment and behavior of social groups within the local church community. Note the larger context of 1 Timothy in which this passage appears:

> I am writing these things to you, hoping to come to you before long; but in case I am delayed, *I write so that you may know how one ought to conduct himself in the household of God,* which is the church of the living God, the pillar and support of the truth (1 Tim. 3:14, 15; italics added).

In the same way every family is governed by certain standards of conduct and principles, the local church family is governed by certain Christian principles of conduct and social arrangement. So in the letter of 1 Timothy, Paul presents distinctly Christian principles of conduct that apply to the household of God. These are not temporary, cultural principles that apply only to the city of Ephesus. They are timeless, universally binding principles for all churches for all times.

**If the men are supposed to be the heads
of the family, they must also be the heads of the
community. The community must be structured
in a way that supports the pattern
of the family.**   STEPHEN CLARK

---

1. Men's prayers.

The priority of prayer in the local church is the topic of 1 Timothy 2:1-7: "First of all, then, I urge that entreaties and prayers, petitions and thanksgivings, be made on behalf of all men, for kings and all who are in authority, so that we may lead a tranquil and quiet life in all godliness and dignity" (1 Tim. 2:1, 2). After stating what is to be done regarding prayer in verses 1-7, Paul exhorts men about prayer, which is part of the larger issue of how a man "ought to conduct [himself] in the household of God" (1 Tim. 3:14). He writes, "Therefore I want the men in every place to pray, lifting up holy hands, without wrath and dissension" (2:8).

Paul wants men to pray "lifting up holy hands, without wrath and dissension." Holy hands stand in contrast to unclean hands, which means sinful hearts that are not acceptable to God. Paul's point is not so much the posture of prayer but the condition of the heart in prayer. The heart of a praying man is to be morally pure. Holiness and prayer, as the Psalmist observes, go together: "If I regard wickedness in my heart, the Lord will not hear" (Ps. 66:18).

To be more specific, men are warned against praying while they harbor an angry disposition toward another. This was particularly important to the church at Ephesus because angry controversies had arisen among the believers as a result of false doctrines. Such warring attitudes seriously hinder the effectiveness of prayer "on behalf of all men" (2:1).

Men and Their Community Responsibility

It is becoming increasingly difficult to find biblically qualified and prepared men to assume the responsibilities of church eldership and deaconship. The hyper-busyness of our culture holds many of our men in a spiritual death grip: "The cult of busyness and activism that infects Christians so much today is one of the greatest barriers to the church becoming what it should be."[89] Too many men have no time for Bible reading, prayer, or church family leadership. Some don't even have time for their families. When men neglect their community leadership responsibilities within the church community, a tragic loss and a stunning victory for the evil one occurs. Our priorities are upside down, and nothing short of radical action will solve the problem. We need to pray and address this problem more intelligently and constructively in our churches, without pouring more guilt on overburdened men.

---

2. Women's dress.

Paul urges women to dress modestly, as motivated by attitudes of Christian propriety and self-restraint. In other words, Paul explains how a woman "ought to conduct [herself] in the household of God" (1 Tim. 3:14, 15). His warning is against expensive, extravagant clothing and elaborate hair-styles (most likely decorated with gold and pearls) that are immodest and inappropriate.

Like Peter, Paul is not prohibiting women from wearing nice clothes, jewelry, or braided hair. His exhortation is against self-display, excess, or the showing off wealth, or the wearing of enticing clothing, all of which are totally inappropriate for godly women. "These words are desperately needed in our culture," says Thomas Schreiner, "for materialism and sexual seductiveness with respect to adornment still plague us."[90]

Instead of being concerned about dressing in expensive clothing, a godly Christian woman should be concerned about "good works." For a woman who professes to walk in close relationship with God, the appropriate dress is a lifestyle of "good works," Christian service, and "deeds of charity."[91] This exhortation is in keeping with the New Testament's overriding description of women's ministry in terms of good works, mercy ministries, loving care, household management, prayer, and gospel witness. "Paul is advocating," writes Knight, "not just modesty in dress, but also that more time and energy be spent on spiritual adornment."[92] Using contemporary imagery, John Stott remarks:

> The church should be a veritable beauty parlour, because it encourages its women members to adorn themselves with good deeds. Women need to remember that if nature has made them plain, grace can make them beautiful, and if nature has made them beautiful, good deeds can add to their beauty.[93]

This exhortation is in keeping with the New Testament's overriding description of women's ministry primarily in terms of good works, mercy ministries, loving care, household management, prayer, and gospel witness.

---

3. Women's submission.

Several years earlier, Paul had written to this same church in Ephesus and instructed wives to submit to their husbands (Eph. 5:22-33). Here, he explains how a woman "ought to conduct [herself] in the household of God." He addresses women's submission in the local church family and shows how it is expressed in the local church. Women, he teaches, whether married or single, are to learn with a submissive spirit. They are not to be the teachers or elders of the congregation.

Here, Paul explains how a woman ought to conduct [herself] in the household of God.

---

a. Learning

The passage states, "A woman must quietly receive instruction with entire submissiveness." Christian women are to master Christian doctrine, be ready to answer anyone who asks about their faith (1 Peter 3:15), and, like Mary, sit at Jesus' feet to learn (Luke 10:38-42). But learning itself is not the issue here. It is assumed that all Christian women will learn the doctrines of the faith. How a woman learns in public, congregational gatherings is the point.

Paul uses two descriptive phrases to explain how she receives teaching: "quietly" and "with entire submissiveness." The Greek noun for "submissiveness" *(hypotagē)* is the noun form of the verb submit *(hypotassō),* the key verb describing the role relationships between husbands and wives (1 Peter 3:1, 5; Eph. 5:21, 22; Col. 3:18; Titus 2:5). A woman is to submit herself in the church family in the way she submits herself in marriage. She is not to take the leadership of the church or to teach the church. Rather, she is to support, encourage, and actively help the men in their leadership role (Gen. 2:18). This is not discrimination against women; it is divine design.

b. Teaching

Verse 12 is the flip side to verse 11. The two verses parallel each other. In the congregational meetings women are to learn Scripture, but they do not take the lead in teaching the church family. This is the men's responsibility.

Paul knew that this crucial issue needed to be stated with authority and straightforward clarity. So he declared with personal apostolic authority in explicit, unambiguous language: "I do not allow a woman to teach or exercise authority over a man, but to remain quiet." How could he have stated this more simply and clearly? In the local church family, women are not to teach or take authority over the men of the church family.

It is important to note that Paul does not absolutely prohibit women from teaching (Acts 18:26; Titus 2:3, 4; 2 Tim. 1:5, 3:14, 15). His prohibition is against women teaching men publicly in the formal church gatherings. Paul

---

**A woman is to submit herself in the church family
in the way she submits herself in marriage.
She is not to take the leadership of the church or to
teach the church. Rather, she is to support,
encourage, and actively help the men in their
leadership role.**

---

makes this distinction because teaching the church is not just a matter of passing on information, it includes exercising authority over those who are taught.

Clark rightly notes that "the Scripture views teaching primarily as a governing function, a function performed by elders, masters, and others with positions of government. In this context, the connection between teaching, exercising authority, and being subordinate can be seen more clearly."[94] Since the woman's role requires subordination, she is not to teach/lead the church.

This passage doesn't imply that women have no ability to teach or lead. We all know that women can be excellent teachers and they can have leadership ability. A Christian woman may be an experienced school teacher, medical doctor, or owner of a business (like Lydia), but when the church assembles, men take the lead in teaching and governing the church family. In this way, the local church displays God's design for the sexes and the concept of headship and submission within the relationship between Christ and His Church.

c. Exercising authority

In addition to the restriction on teaching the church, Christian women are not to "exercise authority over" men in the church. This means they are not to lead or govern the congregation. The Greek word for "exercise authority over" is *authenteō*. This is the fourth key word in the gender debate (the others are *help, submission,* and *head)*. It is highly important because it clearly limits women from serving as pastor elders. The pastoral oversight of the local church is the man's role not the woman's.

Take note: in a letter that presents more teaching on church elders than any other New Testament letter, women are told not to take authority over men. Immediately following his instruction prohibiting women from teaching and leading men (1 Tim. 2:11-15), Paul describes the qualifications for those who oversee (pastor) the local church (1 Tim. 3:1-7). Significantly, the qualifications assume a male subject. Thus the overseer (the same person as pastor or elder) is to be "the husband of one wife" and "one who manages his own household well" (1 Tim. 3:2, 4). Paul gives no suggestion of women elders in this passage on elder qualifications because that is not their God-given role in the church.

Since 1 Timothy 5:17 states that elders lead and teach the church, and since women are not to teach or lead the men of the church, it follows that women cannot be pastor elders in the local church. Thus 1 Timothy 2:8-15 alone should settle the question of female pastor elders.

> **Key word: "To exercise authority over" (Greek, *authenteō*)**
> The Greek term *authenteō* means "to have authority over" or "to exercise

authority." It does not mean "to usurp authority" or "to instigate violence" or "to misuse authority."

Feminist interpreters have created a great deal of controversy regarding this Greek word. They say the verb means to "misuse authority," "instigate violence," "domineer," "thrust oneself," or "usurp authority." Thus they believe Paul forbids women from abusing authority, domineering their male teachers, or trying to usurp men's authority when teaching. They understand the term in a negative way: "a domineering use of authority, rather than merely any use of authority"[95] or "using their authority in a destructive way."[96]

This view of the term *authenteō,* however, is incorrect. In the most up-to-date, in-depth word study of the term *authenteō,* Henry Scott Baldwin, a teacher at Singapore Bible College, has demonstrated that the most likely meaning of the term in this context is "to have authority over."[97]

In addition to Baldwin's exhaustive word study *of authenteō,* Andreas Köstenberger, professor of New Testament at the Southeastern Baptist Theological Seminary, adds an impressive syntactical study of the grammatical sentence structure of verse 11 to help determine the best rendering of the term *authenteō* for the present context.[98] The sentence structure looks like this:

"I do not allow a woman **to teach** [verb 1#] or **exercise authority** [verb 2#] over a man."

Kostenberger shows that the grammatical structure links together the two verbs ("teach" and "exercise authority") in a way that requires them to be either both positive or both negative, not one positive ("to teach," verb 1#) and the other negative ("to wrongfully domineer," verb 2#). Since "to teach" is certainly a positive force, "to exercise authority" must also be a positive one.

The point is this: the second verb must be translated "exercise authority" because it fits the grammatical structure as well as the best usage of the term in this context. Together, the ground-breaking studies by Baldwin and Kostenberger conclude that the best translation *of authenteō* is: "to have (or exercise) authority." This is the translation accepted by the overwhelming majority of Bible commentaries and our major English translations: *The New King James Version, New American Standard Bible. New Revised Standard Version,* and *New International Version.*

d. Biblical reasons

Paul's restriction on women teaching and governing men certainly caused heated criticism, just as it does today. So, as in nearly all other references to distinct male-female roles, Paul immediately supports his instruction with biblical principles and texts: "For it was Adam who was first created, and then Eve. And it was not Adam who was deceived, but the woman being deceived, fell into transgression" (1 Tim. 2:13, 14).

Do not miss this point of argument: Paul bases the restriction on women teaching and governing men directly on the Genesis accounts. Like Jesus, he takes his readers back to the beginning of creation, back to Genesis, back to historical events. He does not appeal to local culture, the lack of women's education, or the supposed problems of heretical female teachers. He simply appeals to God's design as revealed in the Word of God. His argument for restricting women from taking authority over men in the church is based on gender itself as explained in Genesis. Thus, Paul intends his prohibition to be permanent and universally binding on all believers and all churches.

(1) Adam was created first. Paul first appeals to the original creation order in Genesis 2: Adam was created first. Adam's prior creation entails a role of leadership and authority. As the first formed human being, Adam, representing all males, was responsible to be the head in the marriage relationship. This

---

Paul bases the restriction on women teaching and governing men directly on the Genesis accounts. He does not appeal to local culture, the lack of women's education, or the supposed problems of heretical female teachers. He simply appeals to God's design as revealed in the Word of God.

---

headship role is to be displayed in the local church community (an extended family) as well. This explains why women are not "to teach or exercise authority over a man." To do so would contradict God's creation design for the sexes. As the "household of God," the local church must model God's principles.

(2) Adam was not deceived, Eve was. To further prove his point, Paul adds (v. 14) a powerful, negative example. He uses Eve's deception in the garden to illustrate the dangers of male-female role reversals: "And it was not Adam who was deceived, but the woman being deceived, fell into transgression." Adam was not deceived by Satan, Paul says, but Eve was.

In Genesis 3, Satan shrewdly circumvented Adam—the one God created to lead in the relationship—and went directly to Eve, whom he rightly perceived to be the more susceptible of the two to his deceptions. By her own confession, Eve admits deception: "Then the LORD God said to the woman, 'What is this you have done?' And the woman said, 'The serpent deceived me, and I ate'"(Gen. 3:13).

Although God created Adam to be the leader of the couple, Eve acted first, then invited Adam to eat from the forbidden tree. The result of her initiative was not self-improvement but deception, sin, shame, and pain. God's people, therefore, must not take lightly God's order for male and female roles in the family and church. They must heed God's voice when His Word says, "I do not allow a woman to teach or exercise authority over a man."

In verse 15, Paul concludes his line of reasoning about Adam and Eve by qualifying the statement in verse 14 regarding Eve's deception and transgression. Verse 15 literally reads: "But she will be preserved through the bearing of children, if they continue in faith and love and sanctity with self-restraint."

This is a difficult verse to interpret with certainty. But simply put, Paul encourages women to find safety from Satanic deception and to seek fulfillment in their primary calling of mother, wife, and homemaker (1 Tim. 5:14, 15; Titus 2:4, 5), assuming, of course, that they continue in the faith. It is not a woman's calling to govern or teach the church family.

B. 1 Corinthians 14:33*b*-40: Submission in the Church Meetings

First Corinthians 14 is quite similar to 1 Timothy 2, so we need only make a few brief comments on the passage.

Paul wrote 1 Corinthians to the church in the city of Corinth in the year A.D. 56. Some six years later, he wrote 1 Timothy to the church in Ephesus. In both letters, Paul teaches women's submission in the church family and supports his teaching with the Old Testament creation account and his unique authority as an apostle. In 1 Corinthians 14, Paul adds further support for the practice of submission by employing the arguments of the universal practice of all the churches and a commandment of Jesus Christ. Hence, these two pass; should be studied together. They each help to interpret the other.

With 1 Timothy 2 in mind, read the following passage from 1 Corinthians:

14:33*b* as in all the churches of the saints.

14:34   The women are to keep silent in the churches; for they are not permitted to speak, but are to subject themselves, just as the Law also says.

14:35   If they desire to learn anything, let them ask their own husbands at home; for it is improper for a woman to speak in church.

14:36   Was it from you that the word of God first went forth? Or has it come to you only?

14:37   If anyone thinks he is a prophet or spiritual, let him recognize that the things which I write to you are the Lord's commandment.

14:38   But if anyone does not recognize this, he is not recognized.

Because of unruly conduct during congregational meetings by spiritually zealous members, particularly those who spoke in tongues, Paul set forth specific guidelines for order and propriety in the church meeting (vv. 26-35). His final guideline concerns women's participation in the church meeting (vv. 33*b*-38).

What Paul means by "silence" is interpreted in various ways, and it is not necessary for our purpose to resolve the issue here. I have intentionally avoided debatable topics that do not specifically address the equal yet different theme. There are legitimate differences of interpretation over certain passages among complementarians, but these differences do not affect our main topic. We do not want side issues to cloud the fact that God created men and women equal yet different. The point to be made is that Paul again refers to the woman's submission in the church family.

1. The Law and Christianity agree on submission.

The Law of Moses agrees with Christian teaching. Paul seeks in this passage to protect his sisters from conduct that is inappropriate to God's will and design for them. He explains that women's submission will manifest itself in certain specific ways, one of which is in speech and public conduct. Paul uses the doctrine of submission (Greek, *hypotassō)* to support his instruction regarding the woman's role in church meetings. The injunction on submission is Christian teaching, yet it is in full agreement with the Law of God: "for they are.. .to subject themselves, just as the Law also says"(14:34).

To subject themselves, just as the Law also says   PAUL

By the term "Law" Paul means the Law of Moses (1 Cor. 9:8, 9) and specifically Genesis 2. Two chapters earlier, Paul cited Genesis 2 to support his teaching on women's and men's roles: "For man does not originate from woman, but woman from man; for indeed man was not created for the woman's sake, but woman for the man's sake" (1 Cor. 11:8, 9). Paul doesn't need to repeat the same Genesis verses from 1 Corinthians 11:8, 9 in 14:34, so he simply abbreviates them by saying "the Law also says" (see also 1 Tim. 2:13, 14). Please observe that Paul never tires of telling his readers that his gender teachings are rooted soundly in the creation laws of Genesis.

2. Universal church practice agrees with submission.
Paul feels strongly about this issue. He introduces his instruction on women by saying, "as in all the churches of the saints" (v. 33*b*).[99] This universal claim, "in all the churches of the saints," is meant to reinforce his instructions, encourage obedience, and bolster his directive on submission. Specifically, the Corinthian believers are not to act independently of "all" the churches on this doctrine.

The city of Corinth had "a fiercely independent spirit."[100] The church at Corinth adopted some of this unhealthy independence and pride. They were "marching to their own drum."[101] Several times in the letter to the Corinthians, Paul reminds the superior, independent-minded Corinthians of standard apostolic church practices, appealing to them to amend their ways and conform to such practices. Here, he wants them to follow what all the other churches do in regard to women's participation in the church meetings, so this was not a special cultural issue that applied only to the church at Corinth. In verse 36,

---
As in all the churches of the saints   PAUL
---

a good deal of emotion erupts on Paul's part in response to their independent spirit. He is frustrated with their independent, prideful attitude. He fires two stinging questions at them: "Was it from you that the word of God first went forth? Or has it come to you only?" He wants to know if the Word of God originated from their church or was deposited only in their church. These are absurd questions, of course, but Paul wants them to see how absurdly they are thinking and acting. How did they become so independent of the gospel, Paul, and the other churches? Did they think they were the founders of the faith, the mother church, the authors of Scripture, or the sole depository of the truth?

> **Paul reminds the superior, independent-minded Corinthians of standard apostolic church practices, appealing to them to amend their ways and conform to such practices. He wants them to follow what all the other churches do in regard to women's participation in the church meetings.**

In concluding his unwelcome instructions, Paul appeals finally to his unique apostolic authority (vv. 37, 38). "If anyone thinks he is a prophet or spiritual, let him recognize that the *things which I write to you are the Lord's commandment.* But if anyone does not recognize this, he is not recognized" (italics added). Paul had his critics in this church, so he focused directly on those individuals who thought they were prophets or spiritual people. He writes, in effect, "If you are really spiritual people, you will recognize that what I write to you as an authoritative apostle is the Lord's commandment." Commentator Leon Morris observes, "No higher claim could possibly be made."[102]

In stern tone, verse 38 states that anyone who fails to recognize Paul's unique, divine authority is himself not recognized as a spiritual person or prophet—certainly not by God and hopefully not by spiritually discerning believers. The truth is, Paul's words represent Jesus Christ's words. Jesus Christ speaks through Paul. Paul's teaching on the woman's role is the

> **The things which I write to you are the Lord's commandment.   PAUL**

teaching of Jesus Christ on the woman's role. Anyone who claims to be spiritual should know that what Paul writes is Christ's command. "Some of the Corinthians thought they had spiritual discernment. Let them show it by recognizing inspiration when they saw it!"[103]

C. 1 Corinthians 11:2-16: Headship, Submission, and Glory

First Corinthians 11 is not a popular, well-known passage. Yet of the three 1 Corinthian passages addressed in this book, 1 Corinthians 11 is extraordinarily rich in Christology, Christian anthropology, angelology, Old Testament interpretation, gender theology, and interpretive challenges.

Some dissension existed among the Corinthians over the practice of covering and uncovering their heads. Paul wanted the Corinthians to understand the correct theological and biblical bases for covering and uncovering the head, and thus to confirm the good practice of those who held firmly to "the tradition" he had taught them (v. 3).

The passage also mentions women who prophesy. What should be noted here is that the subject of women prophesying is addressed along with the doctrine of male headship. Both truths must be held in tension; one doesn't eliminate the other.

It is a long, complicated passage, so ask your heavenly Father to spark your interest and illuminate your mind to this deeply insightful text. Observe particularly verses 3 and 7:

> **11:2** Now I praise you because you remember me in everything and hold firmly to the traditions, just as I delivered them to you.
>
> **11:3** But I want you to understand that Christ is the head of every man, and the man is the head of a woman, and God is the head of Christ.
>
> **11:7** For a man ought not to have his head covered, since he is the image and glory of God; but the woman is the glory of man.
>
> **11:8** For man does not originate from woman, but woman from man;
>
> **11:9** for indeed man was not created for the woman's sake, but woman for the man's sake.
>
> **11:10** Therefore the woman ought to have a symbol of authority on her head, because of the angels.
>
> **11:11** However, in the Lord, neither is woman independent of man, nor is man independent of woman.
>
> **11:12** For as the woman originates from the man, so also the man has his birth through the woman; and all things originate from God.
>
> **11:16** But if one is inclined to be contentious, we have no other practice, nor have the churches of God.

Using the strongest possible arguments, 1 Corinthians 11 asserts male headship. This passage parallels Ephesians 5 with its firm affirmation and rich demonstration of the doctrine of headship, especially verse 3: "But I want you to understand that Christ is the head of every man, and the man is the head of a woman, and God is the head of Christ." Paul further argues the fact from Genesis 2 that man "is the image and glory of God; but the woman is the glory of man."

First Corinthians 11 doesn't present the headship doctrine as a temporary, first-century accommodation to Greco-Roman culture. Rather, this passage presents the headship doctrine as a permanent, God-ordered arrangement for the sexes. Moreover, as in 1 Corinthians 14, Paul supports what he says with the universal practice of all the churches (v. 16).

1. Three headship-subordination relationships.

Paul launches into his topic with lofty theological fervor: "But I want you to understand that Christ is the head of every man, and the man is the head of a woman, and God is the head of Christ" (v. 3). Through these three pairs of statements (Christ/man, man/woman, God/Christ), Paul affirms that a headship-submission relationship exists between Christ and man, between man and woman, and between God and Christ. These relationships cannot be altered to suit secular society's egalitarian philosophy. The headship relationship between man and woman is not a cultural accommodation; it is divinely planned.

a. Christ/Man

Paul first wants his readers to understand that "Christ is the head of every man." God doesn't exempt the man from being under authority. No man is self-ruling. Every man (male) has a head, a leader, an authority figure to whom he must submit. That head is Christ. Christian women, as well as Christian men, need to know that every man has a head to whom he should submit and obey.

An important lesson for men emerges here. Since Christ is a head, He perfectly models godly headship. Christ never abuses those under His leadership. "Therefore they [men] are not free to define and to exercise their headship in any way they choose, but only according to the pattern of Christ's own headship and in accordance with Christ's teaching about male headship given through the inspired apostles (Eph. 5:23-33; 1 Peter 3:7)."[104]

b. Man/Woman

Second, Paul wants his readers to understand that "the man is the head of a woman." This is not only the center pair of the three statements, it is the main point to the overall context. Some believers in Corinth may have taken their newly found liberty and position in Christ to unbiblical conclusions. So Paul reminds them that a headship-submission relationship exists by design between men and women.[105] In fact, the woman is the only one not called a "head." Man is a head, Christ is a head, and God is a head.

This verse stands in opposition to the feminist viewpoint that woman's submission is a requirement resulting from the Fall (Gen. 3:16) and that one of the results of Christ's work on the Cross was to abolish the curse of the headship-subordination relationship between man and woman. This verse clearly reveals that just as the crucified, risen, and exalted Christ is head of the new creation, Christ is head of the man, God is the head of Christ, and man is the head of the woman. The woman is not inferior to the man because she submits herself to him any more than Christ is inferior to God the Father because He submits Himself to the Father.

The headship-submission relationship of the man and woman is evidenced not only in the original creation order of Genesis but in the greater order of the Godhead. Thus man's headship authority is rooted in God's own nature. Furthermore, the local church of Jesus Christ is to model this headship relationship between man and woman through certain gender-appropriate actions.

c. God/Christ

Third, Paul wants his readers to understand that "God is the head of Christ." By stating that "God is the head of Christ," Paul emphasizes a relationship of authority and subordination between God the Father and God the Son. Christ subordinates Himself to God the Father. Thus Jesus Christ exercises both the role of head and the role of subordinate. He is an example for both sexes.

Jesus Christ exercises both the role of head and the role of subordinate. He is an example for both sexes.

Jesus Christ is God the Son. He is fully and eternally equal with God the Father in essence, power, glory, and worth, yet He is distinct in role and mission. In His mission and role as redeemer, sent by God the Father, He is functionally subordinate to God.[106]

He willingly obeys and submits to God the Father's authority and will (1 Cor. 15:28; see also 3:23). With remarkable precision, S. Lewis Johnson, Jr. former professor at Dallas Theological Seminary, summarizes this truth:

The ultimate and telling proof that equality and submission may coexist in glorious harmony is found in the mediatorial mission of the Son of God, "God from God, Light from Light, true God from true God" (Nicaea), who completed [His mission] in the true liberation of submission to His Father (cf. John 8:21-47; 1 Corinthians 15: 24-28; cf. 11:3).[107]

What a tremendous encouragement this truth is! If Jesus Christ our Lord is submissive and willingly suffered in obedience to the will of His head, so can every Christian man and woman gladly submit to their respective heads, even when it is disagreeable or difficult to do so. *"From this we gather at once what an important thing headship is in the realm of redemption: under God everyone, whether man, woman or Christ himself, has a head* (italics added)."[108]

The ultimate and telling proof that equality and submission may coexist in glorious harmony is found in the mediatorial mission of the Son of God...who completed [His mission] in the true liberation of submission to His Father.   S. LEWIS JOHNSON

---

2. The original order of creation.

In verses 7-12, Paul presents a second line of reasoning to support the covering/uncovering of the head: the Genesis creation account of man and woman. Using the creation account to support men's and women's roles is consistent with what Paul does in similar contexts (1 Cor. 14:34; 1 Tim. 2:12-14; Eph. 5:31, 32). Take a moment to review the following verses:

11:7 For a man ought not to have his head covered, since he is the image and glory of God; but the woman is the glory of man.

11:8 For man does not originate from woman, but woman from man:

11:9 for indeed man was not created for the woman's sake, but woman for the man's sake.

11:11 However, in the Lord, neither is woman independent of man, nor is man independent of woman.

11:12 For as the woman originates from the man, so also the man has his birth through the woman; and all things originate from God.

a. Man is the image and glory of God

Paul states that the man is "the image and glory of God" (v. 7). Not only is man made in God's image, he is also "the glory of God." This is a significant, profound teaching that should not be passed over lightly. Verse 7 deserves some extra thought and attention.

When God made the first human being, He made a male human being. The male of the species was created first and directly by God and was made lord of the earth. Looking back at verse 3, the man is a "head" just as Christ and God are both heads, but this is not true of the woman. Thus the man displays roles that reflect God's roles as head and authority: "Men in their masculinity are like lenses which magnify various attributes of God Himself."[109]

The Glory of God

To be the glory of God means both to display some of God's distinguishing characteristics and to give praise to Him. William E. and Barbara K. Mouser, in their courses entitled *Five Aspects of Man* and *Five Aspects of Woman,* list the following ways in which man is the glory of God.

First, males display the glory of God by their strength and authority in their bearing and physique. "God has given men the glory of strength. Their bones, muscles, and features are bigger, stronger, and more chiseled in appearance. Men's voices are deeper and bespeak authority. The masculine being is characterized by self-possession, decisiveness, and initiative (Prov. 30:29-31). Ultimately, all strength, authority, and power reside in God. He granted to men the honor of displaying these characteristics in their physical bodies and bearing."[110]

Second, males display the glory of God by "sharing with God His masculine roles, roles such as father, son, bridegroom, husband, warrior, king, and priest. Men take these roles by virtue of their created masculinity."[111]

Third, males display the glory of God by leading in worship. "Men were the family patriarchs of the Old Testament and held the offices of priest and king.... The New Testament teaches that men should be elders (1 Tim. 2 and 3), that men should have final responsibility for interpreting and defending Scripture (1 Cor. 14:29-40), and that men and women should observe and show respect for the created order in worship (1 Cor. 11:3-16)."[112]

---

b. Woman is the glory of the man

In contrast, woman is "the glory of the man." Paul carefully avoids saying that woman is the image of man because she is not. The creation narrative expressly states that woman, like the man, was created in the image of God (Gen. 1:27). Both the man and the woman bear God's image, and in this they are equal. However, in their unique gender design and relationship roles, men and women are created differently. Thus the glory of the man and the glory of the woman differ.

From this we gather at once what an important thing headship is in the realm of redemption: under God everyone, whether man, woman or Christ himself, has a head. DAVID GOODING

That the woman is the glory of man is illustrated and proven by the creation account quoted in verses 8 and 9.

(1) Woman from the man. God created Adam first and directly (Gen. 2:7). Out of the side of Adam, God formed Eve (Gen. 2:21). Verse 8 reads: "For man does not originate from woman, but woman from man." Paul states this in a way that emphasizes man's primacy. The woman was formed out of the man's body, so in this sense she is "the glory of man."

Paul uses these same facts concerning the creation order of male and female in 1 Timothy 2:13 to support masculine leadership in the church.

(2) Woman for the man. Paul says in verse 9, "for indeed man was not created for the woman's sake, but woman for the man's sake." Verse 9 refers back to Genesis 2:18, which says God created the woman to be "a helper suitable for him [Adam]." Her role was to help the man, to complement and support him. Thus, "the man's role is not defined in terms of the woman's, but the woman's in terms of the man's."[113] In this also, woman is man's glory.

God created the woman for the man, to be the man's helper and companion. In the way that a beautiful, wise queen is the crowning glory to a king, so is the woman to the man. God created woman to directly reflect the man's headship authority by recognizing it, revealing it, submitting to it, receiving it, and supporting his leadership.

This is not a cultural issue or concept. It is the divine plan. By the woman's very being in the image of God—her beauty, grace, and wisdom; her life-giving powers; her dependence on the man; her sexual responsiveness; her support of his leadership and authority—she is his glory. As the woman is the glory of the man, so too the bride, the Church, is the glory of Christ.

c. The interdependence of man and woman

Paul is sensitive to how easily the issue of male-female distinctions can be misunderstood and abused by sinful people. So in verses 11 and 12 he counterbalances what he has said about the woman being the glory of the man by asserting the interdependence of both sexes.

Man is the head of the woman (v. 3), but he is also dependent on the woman and needs her as much as she needs him (vv. 11, 12). The truths of verses 3 and 7 should never be separated from the truths of verses 11 and 12. Headship and submission must always be taught in connection with the equality and interdependence of the sexes. As the inspired writer says, "in the Lord, neither is woman independent of man, nor is man independent of woman" (v. 11). This dependence on one another is explained in verse 12. Just as Eve was formed out of Adam (she is dependent on him), so also man owes his existence to woman through whom he is born (he is dependent on her).

In addition, "all things originate from God." Both the man and the woman originate equally from the hand of God. He is the Creator who defines our existence and personhood. He is the potter, we are the clay. All are dependent on Him. So let no man or woman act as "Creator" or "Lord" of the other.

Headship and submission must always be taught in connection with the equality and interdependence of the sexes.

The three key New Testament words—"head," "submission," and "exercise authority"—plainly teach the headship-submission doctrine. Paul's instruction regarding this doctrine to the churches at Ephesus, Corinth, Colossae, and on the island of Crete remind us that in a sinful world even Christians struggle with submission and headship. Paul, therefore, had to reaffirm God's original creation design for men and women. Christianity did not abolish God's original design for men and women; it brought it into better focus.

D. Romans 16:1-16; Acts 16:14, 15, 18:24-26; Philippians 4:2, 3; 1 Timothy 3:11: Ministering Women

Although women could not serve as pastor elders among the first churches, they were actively involved in serving the Christian community and evangelizing. They were servants of the Lord and the Lord's people.

1. Romans 16:1-16.

Paul mentions a number of these women at the close of his letter to the Christians in Rome (vv. 1-16). He specifically mentions or greets twenty-nine individuals, of whom at least eight and possibly nine are women: Phoebe; Prisca; Mary; Junias (?); Tryphaena; Tryphosa; Persis; the mother of Rufus; Julia, the sister of Nereus. This passage demonstrates unquestionably that Paul had high regard for women.

These women were Paul's sisters in the Lord, his beloved friends, and fellow workers in the gospel. He is positively delighted to praise them for their noble service, courage, hard work, and love. Their work was a vital and necessary part of the Lord's work. Hence, he valued and acknowledged them.

What an example this should be to us! Far too often sisters who labor for the Lord are unappreciated and go unnoticed. Observe the difference in Paul's attitude as you read this passage:

16:1 I commend to you our sister Phoebe, who is a servant of the church which is at Cenchrea;

16:2 that you receive her in the Lord in a manner worthy of the saints, and that you help her in whatever matter she may have need of you; for she herself has also been a helper of many, and of myself as well.

16:3 Greet Prisca and Aquila, my fellow workers in Christ Jesus,

16:4 who for my life risked their own necks, to whom not only do I give thanks, but also all the churches of the Gentiles;

16:6 Greet Mary, who has worked hard for you.

16:7 Greet Andronicus and Junias, my kinsmen and my fellow prisoners, who are outstanding among the apostles, who also were in Christ before me.

16:12 Greet Tryphaena and Tryphosa, workers in the Lord. Greet Persis the beloved, who has worked hard in the Lord.

16:13 Greet Rufus, a choice man in the Lord, also his mother and mine.

16:15 Greet Philologus and Julia, Nereus and his sister, and Olympas, and all the saints who are with them.

a. Phoebe

The first woman mentioned is Phoebe. Paul enthusiastically recommends her to the Christians in Rome as a Christian sister and "a servant of the church which is at Cenchrea." The Greek term for "servant" is *diakonos.* This is the Greek word for *deacon,* but it is also the ordinary term for *servant* in the general, non-official sense. What Paul means by *diakonos* is uncertain, as either meaning fits the context.

If she was a deacon, Phoebe was involved in an official work of mercy and benevolence, for that is the duty of the New Testament deacon. She would minister to the congregation's poor, its needy widows, and the sick. If by *diakonos* Paul means servant in the general, non-official sense, Phoebe was sacrificially involved in helping the church in all kinds of practical ways: hospitality, financial giving, prayer, witness, teaching other women, counseling, visitation, and benevolence.

Paul also states that she had "been a helper of many, and of myself as well." Some say the Greek term for "helper" *(prostatis)* means a "patron" or " leader,"[114] suggesting that Phoebe was a pastor or leader of the church. This interpretation, however, doesn't fit the context. In the feminine form and the present context, the best rendering is "helper," meaning one who renders assistance.[115]

Paul's request is that the Roman Christians help *(paristēmi)* Phoebe because she had been a "helper" *(prostatis)* to many Christian people including himself. There is some indication that Phoebe was a woman of means. If so, she used her resources to help "many" Christian people including Paul (Rom. 16:2). Paul certainly is not saying she led many people, including himself. The point is, she should be helped because she has helped many others, and he was one of those. All the major English translations render the term in this way.

Phoebe was a worker for the Lord and a leading, influential woman among the Christians in Cenchrea. She was a model of Christian love and service. Nothing in the text, however, suggests that she was an elder, overseer, teacher of the church, or that the church was under her personal care.

b. Prisca (Priscilla)

The second woman mentioned is Prisca, wife of Aquila (v. 3). Both Prisca (also called Priscilla) and Aquila were Paul's "fellow workers in Christ Jesus," which means that they were a husband-wife evangelistic team. Like Paul, they were dedicated to the spread of the gospel. Because of their love and esteem for Paul, they at one time risked their lives to save him from a life-threatening situation, the details of which we are uninformed. Paul was proud to call Priscilla as well as Aquila a fellow worker, a colleague in the gospel mission. As a result of this couple's labors and remarkable courage, Paul and "all the churches of the Gentiles" gave heartfelt thanks for both of them.

c. Mary

Paul greets Mary and acknowledges that she "has worked hard for you" (v. 6). Whatever her labor consisted of, we don't know the details, but Paul had heard of her service on behalf of the Roman Christians. He sincerely appreciated her devotion to the Lord's people and reminds the Roman Christians of her work. She needed to be recognized and appreciated for her work.

d. Junias

There is disagreement over the name and official position of "Junias." Verse 7 reads: "Greet Andronicus and Junias, my kinsmen and my fellow prisoners, who are outstanding among the apostles, who also were in Christ before me." It is debated whether Junias (Greek, *Iounian*) is a woman or a man. If a woman, her name is Junia. If a man, it is Junias.

What rockets this obscure text into high-profile scholarly controversy is that Junias and Andronicus are described as "outstanding among the apostles." Evangelical feminists seize this text as an example of a woman apostle. But there are several reasons why this is not necessarily the case.

First, to be fair with the evidence now available, we cannot say with certainty whether the name *(Iounian)* is a female name or a male name. As one would expect, complementarians favor the male name, Junias, and feminists favor the female name, Junia.

Second, the fact that Jesus Christ directly appointed male apostles only and that all other persons named in the New Testament as apostles are clearly men, should make one cautious of declaring with confidence that this passage proves the existence of female apostles in the New Testament era.

Third, Paul's teaching that a woman is not to "teach or exercise authority over a man," that "the man is the head of a woman," and that women in the congregational meetings "are to subject themselves" does not lend support to the theory of a woman apostle. Indeed, it contradicts it. If we take seriously Paul's overall teaching about the roles of men and women in the family and church, it is hard to believe that his friend Junias is a highly commended woman apostle.

Therefore, it is a surprise when a distinguished commentator such as James Dunn declares, "We may firmly conclude, however, that one of the foundation apostles of Christianity was a woman and wife."[116] Such a statement is wishful thinking, not an unquestionable fact.

e. Tryphaena, Tryphosa, Persis, Rufus's mother

Paul sends greetings to Tryphaena and Tryphosa, who possibly were sisters (v. 12). Paul recognizes them as "workers in the Lord." The kind of work they performed is not defined.

Paul affectionately refers to Persis as "the beloved" (v. 12). The use of the past tense for "worked hard" suggests that she is either an older woman or is ill and her years of hard work are in the past. By serving many, she has become to all "beloved," which is why "she is accorded an eminence not given to Tryphaena and Tryphosa."[117]

The name of Rufus's mother is unknown to us, but it is well known to the Lord (v. 13). This woman treated Paul with such motherly love and care that he felt like her son.

2. Acts 16:14, 15; Philippians 4:2, 3: Lydia, Euodia, and Syntyche.

There were other women with whom Paul worked and gladly praised. In the church at Philippi, the names of three, active, influential women appear: Lydia, Euodia, and Syntyche. Philippians 4:2, 3 reads:

> **4:2** I urge Euodia and I urge Syntyche to live in harmony in the Lord.
> **4:3** Indeed, true companion, I ask you also to help these women who have shared my struggle in the cause of the gospel, together with Clement also and the rest of my fellow workers, whose names are in the book of life.

Of Euodia and Syntyche Paul can say, they "shared my struggle in the cause of the gospel" and were thus considered "fellow workers" (Phil. 4:3). Using a battle metaphor, Paul portrays these two women as fighting at his side for the cause of the gospel in evangelism. Their ministry was important to his unique gospel mission and the church at Philippi. Today we might refer to such women as missionaries.

Lydia was a businesswoman and the first convert in the church at Philippi. She, too, was a dynamic, strong woman. Her home became Paul's home and possibly the meeting place for the church. "What role Lydia actually played in the gathering of believers is pure conjecture."[118] Luke records in Acts 16:14, 15:

> **16:14** A woman named Lydia, from the city of Thyatira, a seller of purple fabrics, a worshiper of God, was listening; and the Lord opened her heart to respond to the things spoken by Paul.

> **16:15** And when she and her household had been baptized, she urged us, saying, "If you have judged me to be faithful to the Lord, come into my house and *stay" And she prevailed upon us* (italics added).

All three of these women had become valued friends of Paul in the gospel mission.

3. Acts 18:24-26: Priscilla, Aquila, and Apollos.

One incident in the ministry of Priscilla and Aquila has raised plenty of discussion. When Priscilla and Aquila first met the powerful evangelist Apollos in Ephesus, they discovered that he was deficient in his understanding of the gospel:

> **18:24** Now a Jew named Apollos, an Alexandrian by birth, an eloquent man, came to Ephesus; and he was mighty in the Scriptures.

> **18:25** This man had been instructed in the way of the Lord; and being fervent in spirit, he was speaking and teaching accurately the things concerning Jesus, being acquainted only with the baptism of John;

> **18:26** and he began to speak out boldly in the synagogue. But when Priscilla and Aquila heard him, they took him aside and explained to him the way of God more accurately.

Commenting on this account, one feminist scholar gleefully announces "a clear indication of authoritative teaching by a woman in the church."[119] This account proves no such "clear indication," however.

Not for one second do we want to minimize Priscilla's knowledge of and devotion to the gospel or her influence on Apollos, for she was a great woman. Yet the text does not clearly indicate that Priscilla taught the church or was an elder. The text, in fact, says nothing about the church. What Luke speaks of is a private meeting between three persons for which no further details are given.

4. First Timothy 3:11: Women as deacons.
Many sound Bible commentators believe that 1 Timothy 3:11 refers to women deacons who serve women.

> **3:11**   Women [or wives] must likewise be dignified, not malicious gossips, but temperate, faithful in all things.

Others, however, understand these "women" to be wives who assist their deacon husbands.[120] But even if they are women deacons, they hold an office of mercy ministries, not one of governance and teaching. Thus, women deacons would not violate Paul's restriction against women leading men.

The Holy Spirit gifts and empowers all believers for ministry—women as well as men. First-century Christian women played an indispensable role in the Lord's work. They were counted, involved, and active during the first days of the Christian movement (Acts 1:14). Yet their active role in advancing the gospel and caring for the Lord's people was accomplished in ways that did not violate the divine pattern of masculine headship in the Church.

According to the New Testament, and dependent upon their individual giftedness, spiritual maturity, and appropriate settings, Christian women should be:

- wholeheartly participating in the work of God, serving God and His people through the spiritual gifts He has given them (1 Cor. 7:34, 11:5, 16:15; Acts 16:15; Rom. 16:1-4,6, 12).
- actively studying and learning the doctrines of Scripture. They should be able to defend their beliefs at any time and to instruct others in the

faith (1 Peter 3:15; Acts 18:26; 1 Tim. 2:11).
- actively witnessing in evangelism (Phil. 4:2, 3; 2 Tim. 1:5).
- engaging in mercy ministries to needy people (Luke 8:1-3; Acts 9:36, 39; 1 Tim. 2:10, 3:11, 5:10, 16; Rom. 16:13).
- serving the local church (Rom. 16:1, 6).
- teaching domestic skills to other women (Titus 2:4, 5).
- showing hospitality (Acts 16:15, 18:3; 1 Tim. 5:10).
- praying and prophesying (1 Cor. 7:5, 11:5; Acts 21:9; 1 Tim. 5:5; Rev. 2:20).
- caring for their husbands and children (1 Tim. 2:15, 5:10, 14; Titus 2:4, 5).

The principle of male headship does not diminish the significance and necessity of a woman's active involvement in the Lord's work. Women are tremendous evangelists, prayer warriors, generation builders, mercy ministers, care-givers, dispensers of wisdom, and lovers of the Lord. Many women have suffered and been martyred for the gospel. We must never forget them, diminish their service to our Lord, or be ungrateful for their contribution.

First-century Christian women played an indispensable role in the Lord's work. They were counted, involved, and active during the first days of the Christian movement.

E. Galatians 3:28: Oneness in Christ

I will close this study lesson with a final text of Scripture, Galatians 3:28. This is a glorious passage for both men and women. Gender makes no difference in terms of salvation and its blessings. Although all Christians heartily agree that this is a stupendous text, it is, unfortunately, a much-fought-over text.

For our feminist brothers and sisters, Galatians 3:28 is the theological starting point for the gender debate. It is the decisive key to interpreting all gender passages. Complementarians object to such claims, however. As you read these verses, focus on verse 28, especially the exhaustively debated phrase, "neither male nor female." Because of the complex way in which Paul unfolds his argument from Old Testament history, it will require extra thought on your part to follow and understand his reasoning. You may want to read the entire context, which includes Galatians 3:1-4:7.

> **3:16** Now the promises were spoken to Abraham and to his seed. He does not say, "And to seeds," as referring to many, but rather to one, "And to your seed," that is, Christ.
>
> **3:17** What I am saying is this: the Law, which came four hundred and thirty years later, does not invalidate a covenant previously ratified by God, so as to nullify the promise.
>
> **3:18** For if the inheritance is based on law, it is no longer based on a promise; but God has granted it to Abraham by means of a promise.
>
> **3:26** For you are all sons of God through faith in Christ Jesus.
>
> **3:27** For all of you who were baptized into Christ have clothed yourselves with Christ.
>
> **3:28** There is neither Jew nor Greek, there is neither slave nor free man, there is neither male nor female; for you are all one in Christ Jesus.
>
> **3:29** And if you belong to Christ, then you are Abraham's descendants, heirs according to promise.

The context in which Galatians 3:28 appears deals specifically with the question of salvation, which is the undisputed central theme of Paul's theology. False teachers (called the Judaizers) had infiltrated the newly planted churches of Galatia. They taught that Gentile Christians needed to obey the Law of Moses to be truly saved (see Acts 15:1). It is this false gospel that Paul refutes in Galatians 3:1-4:7, the general context for our text.

1. The Meaning of Galatians 3:28.

The context in which Galatians 3:28 appears addresses God's plan of salvation; the purpose of the Law; initiation into the promised blessing of Abraham; conditions for receiving salvation, sonship, heirship, and oneness in Christ; and justification by faith apart from the Law of Moses. Thus the point of verse 28 is that the distinctions between male and female, Jew and Greek, slave and freeman are totally irrelevant when it comes to receiving salvation. It is the faith-union with Christ that makes the difference regardless of one's gender, social status, or race.

The man who penned these words had been a strict Pharisaical Jew. Before knowing the good news of Christ, Paul believed that the Abrahamic blessing was for Jews—particularly freeborn, adult, male Jews. Paul's point is that because Christ has come, *all* who believe—not just those who are privileged to be freeborn, Jewish males—are equally qualified to be sons of God, one in Christ, heirs of the blessing of Abraham, and are thus justified and indwelt by the Spirit.

Galatians 3:28 is not intended to address the social evils that can exist between the opposing sides of each of the three contrasting pairs. Paul's point is not the oppressive relationship that can exist between male and female. His point is that in the promised inheritance there is *no distinction* between male and female. How male and female relate to each other after salvation is not the issue here. "What is at stake," writes Cottrell, "is one's spiritual status or relationship with God, not ecclesiastical and societal roles.... The question is how one *enters* into a saving relationship with God, not the ongoing implications of that relationship."[121]

2. The Misuse of Galatians 3:28.

In their euphoria over the phrase "neither male nor female," feminist interpreters stretch Galatians 3:28 far beyond its intended meaning and make exaggerated claims for the text. They declare it to be the mother of all texts on gender, the verse that holds priority over all other gender texts. It is hailed as the "Magna Carta" of Christian feminism and as such abolishes all role distinctions between men and women.

Using the same methods of interpretation that feminists use, Bible-believing homosexuals claim the right to same-sex relationships because the Bible says "neither male nor female." One influential homosexual writer puts it this way: "If there is no longer male and female in Christ Jesus, it does not matter to God which gender we love, which gender we are, or which gender we believe ourselves to be."[122] But does Galatians 3:28 abolish all sexual distinctions? Can men now marry men or women marry women? Can Christians approve of same-sex marriages?

The vast majority of evangelical feminists reject the homosexual viewpoint. They qualify Galatians 3:28 by saying that other passages of Scripture describe homosexuality as a sexual sin (Rom. 1:26, 27; 1 Cor. 6:9, 10) and assert that the phrase "neither male nor female" does not absolutely eliminate all sexual distinctions. Yet when non-feminists qualify Galatians 3:28 with other Scripture texts that teach role differences, feminists cry "foul ball," claiming that such qualifications are contradictions or simplistic interpretations. They want to isolate Galatians 3:28 from further limitations, but their position is inconsistent. Just as Scripture texts regarding homosexual sin qualify Galatians 3:28, so the texts on male-female role differences contradict the egalitarian interpretation of Galatians 3:28.

The same Paul who writes, "there is neither male nor female" also writes, "the husband is the head of the wife, as Christ also is the head of the church." These are not contradictory ideas. The first concept pertains to equality in salvation; the second pertains to husband-wife relationship as created by God. Both truths coexist without contradiction in the New Testament, so we must give equal weight to both. Old Testament scholar Bruce Waltke explains the correct approach to handling both sets of biblical claims: "These truths regarding the equality and inequality of the sexes must be held in dialectical tension, by allowing them the same weight at the same time, and by not allowing one to vitiate the other by subordinating one to the other."[123]

Peter, for example, holds in "dialectical tension" both husband-wife equality and husband-wife role distinctions. The wife, according to Peter, is "a fellow heir of the grace of life" and at the same time is the "submissive" partner in the husband-wife relationship (1 Peter 3:1-7). We can understand biblical gender correctly only when we allow the Scriptures to speak with full authority both on male-female equality as well as on male-female role differences. Feminists, on the other hand, promote a half-truth. They emphasize the equality side of the male-female relationship without recognizing the headship-subordination side.

The reason for the feminist's interpretation is that equality is the feminists' foundational concept. Thus feminists reject that God created both unequal

---

We can understand biblical gender correctly only when we allow the Scriptures to speak with full authority both on male-female equality as well as on male-female role differences.

---

as well as equal dimensions to the sexes. Because they believe so fiercely in pure equality, a submission-headship relationship can only be interpreted as unjust and unfair. But their idea of equality is a secular concept, not a biblical concept, and it destroys God's original ordering of the man-woman relationship, which is characterized by headship among equals.

3. The Implications of Galatians 3:28.

There are important, everyday, social implications to oneness in Christ. People of vastly different racial and social backgrounds and unequal status are brought together in the household of God. All Christians—Jews and Greeks, slaves and free men, males and females—are baptized and indwelt by the Spirit. They are gifted to serve the Body and are full members of the Body of Christ. All are one and need to sacrificially love and serve one another.

Jewish Christians are to exhibit brotherly love for their Gentile brothers and sisters, and vice versa. They are to serve one another, accept one another, eat together and share complete social fellowship. To sever table fellowship because of race was to deny the gospel (see Gal. 2:11-14). "Therefore, accept one another, just as Christ also accepted us to the glory of God" (Rom. 15:7).

Slaves and freemen are to serve one another in love and to view each other according to their new status in Christ. "For he who was called in the Lord while a slave, is the Lord's freedman; likewise he who was called while free, is Christ's slave" (1 Cor. 7:22). Master and slave are to treat one another honorably.

Christian husbands are to love their wives with Christ's selfless, self-sacrificing love. They are not to act as lords over their wives because Christ alone is Lord. A wife is to be treated as "a fellow heir of the grace of life." The wife has authority over her husband's body just as he has authority over hers (1 Cor. 7:4). Christian women as well as men serve in spreading the gospel and serving the Body of Christ.

The plain fact is, Galatians 3:28 within its context does not address husband-wife roles nor does it address male-female roles in the church family. Equality of the sexes is not the point. The Bible says very little about equality, but much about oneness and unity. Jesus, in fact, prayed for our oneness, not our equality (John 17). Regardless of one's gender, race, or social status, mutual love, honor, servanthood, and oneness are to mark members of the new community in Christ. All parties are equally responsible to manifest the life of Christ one to another. Pride of race, heritage, social standing, or gender is sin and must be confessed as such and rejected as incompatible with the character of the Christian community.

Slavery and Gender Distinctions

It is often argued that just as slavery has been eliminated in the Western world as a result of Christian principles, women should be freed

from submission to husbands and church elders. But the parallels between these institutions are not the same.

Role distinctions between the sexes are based on the abiding order of
creation (Gen. 2) and redemption in Christ (Eph. 5). Thus when Paul and
Peter argue for headship and submission, they can base their teaching on
Scripture and God's creation design. These roles are God's will for men
and women.

Slavery, however, is not part of the original order of creation. It is
a human invention. Like divorce, God permitted it (Matt. 19:8). The
apostles provided instruction to guide Christian slaves and masters who
were part of the present social order. Paul's instructions lifted the status
of slaves when he said: "Masters, grant to your slaves justice and fairness, knowing that you too have a Master in heaven" (Col. 4:1). Paul
reminded the Christian slave owner Philemon that his newly converted
slave, Onesimus, was "a beloved brother," and that Philemon should accept Onesimus back as he would Paul himself (Philem. 16, 17).

Paul and Peter do not defend slavery from the Scriptures as they do
headship and submission. Since slavery is a human institution and not
part of the original creation order like marriage, Paul can say to slaves,
"if you are able also to become free, rather do that" (1 Cor. 7:21). Slavery
and marriage are not comparable institutions.

Questions

1. In what ways do one's beliefs in the roles of husbands and wives in Christian
    marriage influence one's beliefs in the roles of men and women in the local
    church family?

2. What general terms best describe the primary ministries God has ordained
    for women? List some verses to support your answers.

3. Does Paul's prohibition against women teaching mean that women have no
    ability to teach or lead others? Explain your answer.

4. Explain the debate between feminists and complementarians over the
    definition of the Greek word *(authenteō)* for "exercise authority." In what
    ways does the sentence structure help define this important Greek word?

5. What biblical arguments does Paul use to support the restriction against

women teaching and governing the local church?

6.   What arguments does Paul use in 1 Corinthians 14:33b-38 to support his teaching on women's submission in the church?

7.   According to 1 Corinthians 11, what can we learn from the fact that God is the "head" of Christ? In what ways does this fact impact our understanding of man's headship and women's submission in marriage?

8.   What important evidence that equality and role differences can coexist in harmony do you find in 1 Corinthians 11?

9.   In what unique ways are men the "glory of God"? In what unique ways is a woman the "glory of the man"?

10.   What can men learn from Paul in Romans 16 about appreciating the spiritual labors of their sisters in Christ?

11.   List specific ministries in which first-century Christian women were engaged.

12.   Why is Galatians 3:28 so important to evangelical feminists?

13.   Does Galatians 3:28 abolish all sexual distinctions? If it does, what would be some of the consequences of this interpretation?

14.   Feminists use the abolishment of slavery as an analogy for advocating the abolishment of the headship and submission relationship in marriage and the church. Is this a correct parallel? If not, why not?

15.   What new information did you learn from this chapter? How will this information help shape your thinking and actions?

V. JESUS CHRIST AND HIS APOSTLES SPOKE PLAINLY

W hat you've taught me so far sounds right, but when I talk to my feminist friends at school, they're constantly accusing me of interpreting the Bible too literally and simplistically."

"You've hit on a highly crucial issue, Tom. I have far too much regard for the Bible to treat it simplistically. I also have too much regard for the Bible to force an interpretation on it or to explain away an obvious teaching by means of erroneous cultural arguments."

"I know exactly what you're saying," Tom responds. "I've heard feminist interpretations that are totally forced interpretations. But what is the solution? How do we really know we have interpreted the Bible correctly?"

"Tom, all Bible-believing Christians claim the Bible to be God's voice speaking to us, or as J. I. Packer puts it: 'The Bible is God preaching.' So in our studies together we have tried to allow God's words to speak for themselves. We have allowed the plain, natural, straightforward meaning of Scripture to be heard. Furthermore, we have allowed the whole of God's Word to speak to us and have been sensitive to the context and culture in which core passages appear. In short, we have used good, sound, time-proven principles of Bible interpretation."

"Could you expand on these principles a bit more?" Tom asks.

"Of course. Here's why I believe that we complementarians have allowed the Bible to speak for itself and why we can be confident that we have interpreted the Bible accurately.

A. We Allow Jesus to Speak and Act for Himself

Jesus Christ prayerfully chose twelve male apostles in accordance with the will of God the Father. Jesus knew perfectly well the long-term consequences of His choice of an all-male apostolate. He did not give in to the spirit of

His age when He appointed male apostles as the eternal foundation stones of His Church (Matt. 19:28; Eph. 3:20; Rev. 21:14). Jesus not only chose male apostles during His time on earth, but, after His resurrection when He was exalted in heaven at God's right hand, He personally chose Matthias, Judas' replacement, and Paul, "a preacher and an apostle...a teacher of the Gentiles" (1 Tim. 2:7).

Jesus knew perfectly well the long-term consequences of His choice of an all-male apostolate.

Since feminists are not happy with Jesus' choice of an all-male apostolate they feel compelled to provide an excuse for His choice. To justify such an embarrassing situation, they say the time wasn't ripe for Jesus to appoint female apostles. They claim that Jesus had to accommodate His choices to the prevailing mood of the day or be rejected. But the Bible suggests no such situation. By making this assumption, feminists bring into question Jesus' character and choices. They render Him irrelevant to the debate on gender. At least on this issue, they insult His courage and integrity.

B. We Allow the Whole of Scripture to Speak for Itself

The Bible, in its entirety, teaches both the equality of the sexes and gender role differences. There are texts that teach equality of the sexes as well as texts that teach specific, gender-based role differences. All of these texts must be allowed to speak with full authority and to be part of the interpretive process.

To eliminate even one text from the discussion on gender is to distort Scripture's complete teaching. The best commentary on the Bible is the Bible itself, and if the whole of Scripture is allowed to speak for itself and interpret itself, we must conclude that Scripture teaches both gender equality and differences. *Complementarians accept both truths as the whole truth.*

Feminists and non-feminists agree that the Bible teaches that men and women are created equal in the image of God and thus are equal in dignity, worth, and personhood. But feminists and non-feminists divide over the texts that teach headship and submission or headship and helper in the relationship between the sexes. Therefore most of the debate revolves around the interpretation of these texts.

Feminists pit one group of texts on women's submission against another group of verses on women's equality and choose the latter to represent the whole truth, which distorts the truth. Complementarians on the other hand, accept both truths as the whole truth.

Feminists are concerned about gender equality only while God is concerned about both gender equality and gender differences. Because feminists reject biblical headship and submission, they advocate a half-truth. They pit one group of texts on women's submission against another group of verses on women's equality and choose the latter to represent the whole truth, which distorts the truth.

Feminists admit that there are some nagging, "obscure" verses that seem to teach headship and submission, but a comprehensive look at the Bible, they say, teaches equality and thus takes precedence over a few disagreeable verses. But their claims ring untrue. Seven specific didactic (teaching) texts teach headship and submission: 1 Peter 3:1-7; Ephesians 5:22-33; Colossians 3:18, 19; 1 Timothy 2:8-15; Titus 2:4, 5; 1 Corinthians 11:1-16, 14:34-38. These are not isolated texts. These are not obscure texts. They are foundational doctrinal texts that intentionally address male-female relationships and roles in the home and church. These texts strongly argue, from the Genesis 2 creation account and from the redemption story of Christ and His Church, that headship and submission are divinely planned by God.

When we look at the whole of the New Testament, we readily see the truth of these seven key passages being implemented in practical ways. Jesus chose twelve male apostles, for example. The prominent leaders and preachers of the Book of Acts are all men: Peter, John, Barnabas, Stephen, Philip, Paul, James the brother of John, James the brother of the Lord, Silas, Timothy, and Apollos. The five teachers and prophets in the church at Antioch named by Luke are men: Barnabas, Simeon, Lucius, Manaen, and Saul (Acts 13:1). The great apostle to the Gentiles is Paul. All the authors of the New Testament, as well as the Old Testament, are men.

Despite these examples and direct commands related to headship and submission, one well-respected commentator and evangelical feminist says, "the Holy Spirit is 'gender-blind.' "[124] Is it not the scholar himself who is blind?

Feminists, in fact, place the Bible at war with itself. They create dishar-
mony and confusion. If the whole Bible is allowed to speak for itself and
interpret itself, it teaches both the equality of the sexes and specific, gender-
based role distinctions.

C. We Allow the Plain Sense of Scripture to Speak for Itself

We affirm that the literal, plain-sense interpretation of Scripture leads to the
conclusion that Jesus and His apostles taught the equality of the sexes and
gender-based role differences. In the most natural, straightforward, plain-
speech manner, the New Testament adamantly insists on the headship-submission relationship for Christian men and women. For example, the three
key New Testament words we have studied—"head," "submission," and "exercise authority"—when allowed their natural meaning in context, affirm the
headship-submission doctrine and utterly refute biblical feminism as false
and deceitful.

Not only do the apostles Paul and Peter expressly state the headship-submission doctrine, they argue cogently and passionately for it, supporting the
timeless universal application of their teaching from the original creation
order and the order of redemption (Eph. 5:23-32; 1 Cor. 11:3). God could not
have been more clear and direct in expressing His mind on this topic.

Protestants have always believed that ordinary believers can understand
the general, plain sense of the Bible. The inspired biblical writers sought to
be understood; they were not trying to be esoteric or to play word games with
their readers. They wrote in intelligible language in order to communicate
God's words in a way that would be understood by ordinary people. One
theologian has aptly said that the plain, literal interpretation of Scripture "is
the basic way in which we let God be God and let God speak."[125] Moreover,
by the plain-sense (literal) interpretation of Scripture, we are able to test and
expose false beliefs and subtle counterfeit doctrines that depend upon distorted methods of interpretation.

Add to this the fact that the New Testament teaching on gender is a simple
doctrine. It is not complex such as prophetic doctrine or the doctrine of the
Holy Trinity. It is basic, bread-and-butter, daily-life doctrine. All believers
should be able to understand, at least in its most general form, what the Bible
teaches on headship and submission. One should not have to be a Ph.D. or a
specialist in hermeneutics (the science of interpretation) to understand headship and submission.

Evangelical feminists, however, have created a confusing, interpretive nightmare regarding this topic. They employ various methods of interpretation and cannot agree among themselves on a single method of interpretation to explain away the headship-submission texts. The one point they whole-heartedly agree upon is that these texts cannot mean what they say. Feminist interpreters thereby demean the plain, straightforward meaning of Scripture and declare the literal interpretation of the headship-submission passages to be simplistic and traditionalistic. As a result, they rob the Bible of its ability to communicate to ordinary people.

The fundamental issue and danger of evangelical feminism lies in its methods of interpreting the Bible.

The fundamental issue and danger of evangelical feminism lies in its methods of interpreting the Bible. These methods seriously undermine the credibility, integrity, and authority of God's written Word. They make the Bible an utterly confusing book, an unsolvable puzzle. The next generation or two will reap the damage done to the Bible's credibility as many other unacceptable doctrines are redefined by these clever, new methods of inter-pretation.

The Bible is not guilty of saying one thing and meaning another. It says what it means. When the plain sense of the Bible is violated, as feminists have done, we are left only with nonsense. Who can trust a Bible that says one thing but means another?

D. We Allow the Core Passages to Speak for Themselves

When constructing any doctrinal position, we should go first to the central, core passages and books of Scripture that present the doctrine in question. For example, the core texts related to the doctrine of salvation are in the books of Romans and Galatians. Complementarians build their doctrine on gender upon the core passages that systematically and directly address men and women in the home and church. There are seven, core didactic passages: 1 Corinthians 11 and 14; Ephesians 5; Colossians 3; 1 Timothy 2; Titus 2; and 1 Peter 3. These core passages of Scripture teach both the equality of the sexes and gender-based role differences.

**When constructing any doctrinal position,
we should go first to the central, core passages and
books of Scripture that present the
doctrine in question.**

Evangelical feminists, in contrast, do all in their power to neutralize these texts. They contend that the seven specific passages on headship and submission are "obscure," "isolated," "problematic," "painfully puzzling," "culturally limited," "not authentic" or should be interpreted "in light of Galatians 3:28," which they consider to be the clearer, more theologically pertinent text. Feminist interpreters declare an all-out war on every word, phrase, sentence, or book that mentions headship and submission. They freely dispose of any text by waving their cultural magic wand and declaring the text to be "cultural," "temporary," or "a first-century custom," which, they insist, makes it irrelevant for people today. Rebecca Groothuis, for example, insists that the texts that teach headship and subordination are "a temporary accommodation to certain functional differences between men and women in ancient patriarchal cultures."[126]

The seven passages on submission and headship mentioned above, however, are not isolated, obscure texts, nor are they culturally conditioned. They are essential building blocks to a comprehensive doctrinal position on gender. They are the didactic, foundational passages on manhood and womanhood for the new covenant people of God.

What is so terribly unsettling to complementarians is that the *New Testament is absolutely clear in its repeated, consistent declarations on headship and submission.* Note again the key phrases used in the core passages:

- "wives, be submissive to your own husbands"
- "the holy women...used to adorn themselves, being submissive to their own husbands"
- "live with your wives in an understanding way, as with someone weaker" (1 Peter 3:1, 5, 7)
- "wives, be subject to your own husbands, as to the Lord" the husband is the head of the wife, as Christ also is the head of the church"
- "as the church is subject to Christ, so also the wives ought to be to their husbands in everything"

- "husbands, love your wives" (Eph. 5:22-25)
- "wives, be subject to your husbands, as is fitting in the Lord"
- "husbands, love your wives" (Col. 3:18, 19)
- "A woman must quietly receive instruction with entire submissiveness"
- "I do not allow a woman to teach or exercise authority over a man" (1 Tim. 2:11, 12)
- "encourage the young women... [to be] subject to their own husbands" (Titus 2:5)
- "the man is the head of a woman"
- "he is the image and glory of God; but the woman is the glory of man"(1 Cor. 11:3, 7)
- "The women are to...subject themselves" (1 Cor. 14:34)

Furthermore, *the apostles use the strongest conceivable arguments to prove headship and submission:* (1) the creation laws of Genesis, (2) the universal practice of the churches, (3) the order within the Godhead, (4) the command of Jesus Christ, and (5) the Christ-Church relationship. Paul is adamant about headship and submission. In fact, he is much stronger about this matter than any of us would want to admit. Again, note the powerful arguments used to support the headship and submission doctrine:

- "the holy women also...being submissive to their own husbands"
- "just as Sarah obeyed Abraham" (1 Peter 3:5, 6)
- "be subject to your own husbands, as to the Lord"
- "the husband is the head of the wife, as Christ also is the head of the church"
- "as the church is subject to Christ, so also wives ought to be to their husbands"
- "love your wives, just as Christ also loved the church" (Eph. 5:22-25)
- "be subject to your husbands, as is fitting in the Lord" (Col. 3:18)
- "Adam who was first created, and then Eve"
- "it was not Adam who was deceived, but the woman being deceived, fell into transgression" (1 Tim. 2:13, 14)
- "I want you to understand that Christ is the head of every man, and the man is the head of a woman, and God is the head of Christ."
- "he is the image and glory of God; but the woman is the glory of man."

- "For man does not originate from woman, but woman from man"
- "man was not created for the woman's sake, but woman for the man's sake"
- "if one is inclined to be contentious, we have no other practice, nor have the churches of God" (1 Cor. 11:3, 7-9, 16)
- "as in all the churches of the saints"
- "subject themselves, just as the Law also says"
- "the things which I write to you are the Lord's commandment"
- "if anyone does not recognize this, he is not recognized" (1 Cor. 14:33, 34, 37, 38)

Even so, some feminists talk as if this doctrine never existed among the apostles and that nearly all Christians since the time of the apostles have misinterpreted the apostles, except, of course, themselves. They explain away the obvious. They work frantically to reinterpret the core passages so that they can enhance gender neutrality. This is nothing but gender-bias interpretation. D. A. Carson, research professor of New Testament at Trinity Evangelical Divinity School, expresses perfectly what many complementarians feel when he writes, "We are facing an ideology that is so certain of itself that in the hands of some, at least, the text is not allowed to speak for itself."[127]

The apostles use the strongest conceivable arguments to prove headship and submission: (1) the creation laws of Genesis, (2) the universal practice of the churches, (3) the order within the Godhead, (4) the command of Jesus Christ, and (5) the Christ-Church relationship. Paul is adamant about headship and submission.

—‌⁊❧—

Questions

1. What does the word *hermeneutics* mean? Use a dictionary to help you answer this question.

2. Why have the methods of interpretation become a major part of the gender debate?

3. What "magic wand" of interpretation do feminists wave over any verse of Scripture in order to eliminate its application for people today? Cite an example using one of the seven core passages.

4. Who do you believe has interpreted correctly the reasons for Jesus' appointment of an all-male apostate—complementarians or feminists? Explain your answer.

5. Why is it necessary to consider the whole of Scripture in order to interpret any doctrine of Scripture accurately? List your reasons.

6. What is meant by the plain, literal sense of Scripture? When interpreting Scripture, why must you always seek the plain, literal, sense of the Scripture?

7. In what ways do the methods of interpretation used by feminists undermine the credibility, integrity, and authority of God's written Word?

8. The author states: "The next generation or two will reap the damage done to the Bible's credibility as many other unacceptable doctrines are redefined by these clever, new methods of interpretation." List doctrines other than gender that you think might be redefined and reinterpreted in the future so that they may be more acceptable to secular society.

9. What does the author mean when he speaks of the "core passages" of a doctrine?

10. Of the seven, core New Testament passages on gender distinctions (headship submission), which two do you find most convincing? Explain your choices.

11. What evidence would you use to prove that Paul is adamant about the headship-submission doctrine?

12. After reading Chapter Five, do you believe that complementarians have interpreted the Scriptures too simplistically, as feminists claim? Explain your answer.

13. What new information did you learn that will help shape your thinking and actions?

VI. Take Courage and Stand Strong in Your Faith

I'm sure glad we took the time to study the Scriptures together," Tom comments. "I didn't realize how much the Bible says about gender. I didn't know how clear it is about this subject. That's what has impressed me the most."

"Tom, let me repeat what I've been saying all along. If the Bible is allowed to speak for itself, it plainly teaches that God created men and women equal in His divine image but different in their respective role functions. One has to twist the Scriptures to eliminate gender role differences from the Bible."

"You're right, but people believe in gender equality so strongly that they won't accept role differences no matter who says it."

"I know! We're standing against a worldwide wave of opinion."

"It's tough to stand against the tide," Tom says.

"True, but we've been called to be faithful to Jesus Christ and His Word, not to popular opinion."

"Pray that I'll have the courage to stand for what I believe."

"I will. Here are some final thoughts to encourage and strengthen your faith."

First, if you believe God created men and women as equal yet different, you stand firmly on sound, honest biblical scholarship. You are faithful to the biblical record. You allow God to speak for Himself and the Bible to say what it means. You protect the Bible's credibility to speak plainly. You believe what God's people have believed since the beginning of human history. You follow in the footsteps of Jesus Christ and His holy apostles. So be encouraged. "Heaven and earth will pass away," Jesus said, "but My words will not pass away" (Matt. 24:35).

Second, some top evangelical, Bible-believing scholars are boldly speaking out against the unsound interpretive methods and conclusions of feminist scholars. They are producing exciting new books and journal articles that challenge feminist strongholds and confirm the truth that the Bible teaches headship and submission. If you are open-minded and seek biblical truth on gender, vital, new research information is now at hand for you to study.[128] So "be diligent to present yourself approved to God as a workman who does not need to be ashamed, *accurately handling the word of truth"* (2 Tim 2:15; italics added).

Third, in spite of the overwhelming cultural pressure to obliterate God-created, gender-defined role differences, millions of local churches and Christian leaders worldwide adamantly refuse to bow the knee to the false idol of egalitarianism. They refuse to accept feminist notions of equality—not because they are wooden-headed literalists, blind traditionalists, or because they fear women—but because God says something different. They also recognize this debate for what it really is—spiritual warfare over the Creator's sovereign design for marriage, the family, the church family, and godly manhood and womanhood:

> For our struggle is not against flesh and blood, but against the rulers, against the powers, against the world forces of this darkness, against the spiritual forces of wickedness in the heavenly places (Eph. 6:12).

Take courage from the strength, faithfulness, and uncompromising courage of your brothers and sisters to follow the Word of the Lord, and to be truly counter-cultural.

Fourth, those who follow God's blueprint for marriage will build happier, stronger marriages, and their children will benefit. Those who know God's plan for marriage and the sexes can help protect their families from a secularized culture that is super-saturated with rebellion against God's laws, with sexual promiscuity, with divorce, fatherlessness, lies, loneliness, and heartache. Furthermore, following God's design for gender will help keep churches doctrinally strong and enable them to grow according to God's plan. So, I say, as the Lord said to Joshua, "This book of the law shall not depart from your mouth, but you shall meditate on it day and night, so that you may be careful to do according to all that is written in it; for then you will make your way prosperous, and then you will have success" (Josh 1:8).

Fifth, complementarians will not give up appealing to our feminist brothers and sisters. Minds have been changed. Unlike secular and theologically liberal feminists, evangelical feminists believe God to be the author of Scripture, God's book. This provides us substantial common ground on which to continue to communicate and persuade. Thus we want to appeal to our feminist brothers and sisters and warn you as friends. The best minds can be blinded by egalitarian philosophy that looks fair and just but contradicts the Creator's decision to make people the way He has.

Sixth, those who follow God's plan for the sexes, marriage, and the church family glorify God. By following His plan, they allow God to be sovereign Lord over His creation. This brings God pleasure, and nothing is more important to a child of God than that.

ENDNOTES

1   William Manchester, "A World Lit Only By Change," *U. S. News & World Report* (October 25, 1993), 6.

2   Richard N. Ostling, "The Second Reformation," *Time* (November 23, 1992), 53.

3   Donald S. Whitney, *Spiritual Disciplines for the Christian Life* (Colorado Springs: NavPress, 1991), 28. Whitney's information is taken from a 1980 *Christianity Today-Gallup* Poll survey. See Harold O. J. Brown, "What's the Connection Between Faith and Works?" *Christianity Today* (October 24, 1980), 26-29.

4   George Gallup, Jr. and Robert Bezilla, *The Role of the Bible in American Society,* On the Occasion of the 50th Anniversary of National Bible Week, November 18-25, 1990 (Princeton: The Princeton Religion Research Center, 1990).

5   "Bible reading will decline in the years ahead. Accordingly, people will be less likely to treat the Bible as their authority in matters of faith and practice. On what alternative will they rely? While there are several possibilities, one of the most likely is personal experience" (Millard J. Erickson, *Where is Theology Going?: Issues and Perspectives on the Future of Theology* [Grand Rapids: Baker, 1994], 100).

6   René Pache, *The Inspiration and Authority of Scripture,* trans. Helen I. Needham (Chicago: Moody, 1969), 221.

7   Emily MacFarquhar, "The War Against Women," *U. S. News & World Report* (March 28, 1994), 42.

8   *The United Nations and the Advancement of Women 1945-1996,* The United Nation Blue Books Series, vol. 6 (rev.ed., New York: Department of Public Information, United Nations, 1996), 57.

9   *The Quotable Kofi Annan: Selections from Speeches and Statements by the Secretary-General* (New York: United Nations, 1998), 31.

10 *Human Development Report 1998,* for the United Nations Development Programme (New York: Oxford University Press, 1998), 16.

11 Ibid., 17.

12 *The World's Women 1995: Trends and Statistics,* Social Statistics and Indicators, Series K, No. 12 (New York: United Nations, 1995), 151-175; *Human Development Report 1998,* for the United Nations Development Programme (New York: Oxford University Press, 1998), 25.

13 *Human Development Report 1993,* for the United Nations Development Programme (New York: Oxford University Press, 1993), 31.

14 Ibid., 17.

15 Barbara Ehrenreich, "For Women, China Is All Too Typical," *Time* (September 18, 1995), 130.

16   Stephen B. Clark, *Man and Woman in Christ: An Examination of the Roles of Men and Women in Light of Scripture and the Social Sciences* (Ann Arbor: Servant, 1980), 5.

17   If you have questions about gender-inclusive language and Bible translation, read Wayne Grudem, *What's Wrong with Gender-Neutral Bible Translations?* (Libertyville: CBMW, 1997); Vern Poythress, "Searching Instead for an Agenda-Neutral Bible," *World* (November 21,1998), 24, 25. Taking issue with them is D. A. Carson, *The Inclusive Language Debate: A Plea for Realism* (Grand Rapids: Baker, 1998).

18   Raymond C. Ortlund, Jr. "Male-Female Equality and Male Headship: Genesis 1-3, " in *Recovering Biblical Manhood and Womanhood: A Response to Evangelical Feminism* (Wheaton: Crossway, 1991), 98.

19   Derek Kidner, *Genesis: An Introduction and Commentary,* Tyndale Old Testament Commentaries (Downers Grove: InterVarsity, 1967), 65.

20   Mary Stewart Van Leeuwen, *Gender & Grace: Love, Work & Parenting in a Changing World* (Downers Grove: InterVarsity, 1990), 42.

21   Rebecca Merrill Groothuis, *Good News for Women: A Biblical Picture of Gender Equality* (Grand Rapids: Baker, 1997), 35.

22   Gilbert Bilezikian, *Beyond Sex Roles: What the Bible Says About a Woman's Place in Church and Family,* 2nd ed. (Grand Rapids: Baker, 1985), 41.

23   Jack Cottrell, *A Critique of Feminist Biblical Interpretation, Gender Roles & The Bible: Creation, the Fall, & Redemption* (Joplin: College Press, 1994), 80.

24   Ibid., 81.

25   Steven Goldberg, *Why Men Rule: A Theory of Male Dominance* (Chicago: Open Court, 1993).

26   Feminists ridicule the prior creation argument by insisting that animals would then have authority over Adam and Eve because they were created first. But this is faulty logic. It is mixing apples and oranges. Only within the human species is the point of prior creation exhibited and explained by the biblical writers. Humans, not animals, were commanded by God to rule the earth. Feminists deny the New Testament interpretation of Adam's prior creation that is expressed in 1 Timothy 2:13.

27   Michael Harper, *Equal and Different: Male and Female in Church and Family,* 2nd ed. (London: Hodder & Stoughton, 1997), 22.

28   Allen P. Ross, *Creation & Blessing: A Guide to the Study and Exposition of Genesis* (Grand Rapids: Baker, 1988), 150.

29   Ward Gasque, "The Role of Women in the Church, in Society and in the Home," *Priscilla Papers* 2:2 (Spring, 1988), 7.

30   Werner Neuer, *Man and Woman in Christian Perspective,* trans. Gordon J. Wenham (Wheaton: Crossway, 1991), 75.

31   Some interpreters contend that this "desire" is a sexual/psychological desire for the man despite the pain of childbirth and even harsh husbandly demands. In other words, a woman needs a man; she finds herself emotionally dependent on a man even though he makes life painful for her. She is thus easily victimized by a man because of her intense desire for one. Others think that the "desire" is a normal, affectionate desire for her husband,

but what she will find that she will get in return is not a lover but a ruler and lord.

A very popular interpretation of the term "desire" claims that the woman's "desire" is a grasping desire to possess or control her husband. The desire is not a desire to submit to her husband, but to rule him, to try to usurp her husband's leadership. The woman manipulates the man to get her way.

Note: the husband is not commanded to dominate the wife. This passage cannot be used to justify male abuse of women. Whether his rule is loving or harsh is not indicated.

32   Cottrell, *Gender Roles & The Bible*, 141.

33   Gordon J. Wenham, *Genesis 1-15*, Word Biblical Commentary (Waco: Word, 1987), 82, 83.

34   The story of Deborah is the exception that proves the rule. See Judges 4:8, 9; 5:2, 7; cf. Isa.3:12.

35   Neuer, *Man and Woman in Christian Perspective*, 87.

36   Groothuis, *Good News for Women*, 109.

37   Ibid., 113.

38   Aída Besancon Spencer, *Beyond the Curse: Women Called to Ministry* (Nashville: Thomas Nelson, 1985), 22.

39   Cottrell, *Gender Roles & The Bible*, 166.

40   John F. Walvoord, *Jesus Christ Our Lord* (Chicago: Moody, 1969), 64, 65.

41   Cottrell, *Gender Roles & The Bible*, 168.

42   William Mouser, *Searching for the Goddess: An Answer to Religious Feminist* (Waxahachie: International Council for Gender Studies, 1980), 17.

43   Gretchen Gaebelein Hull, *Equal To Serve: Women and Men Working Together Revealing the Gospel* (Grand Rapids: Baker, 1987, 1991), 286.

44   Neuer, *Man and Woman*, 96.

45   Groothuis, *Good News for Women*, 21; Paul Jewett, *Man as Male and Female: A study in Sexual Relationships from a Theological Point of View* (Grand Rapids: Eerdmans, 1975), 169.

46   All the New Testament apostles who are clearly named are not only male but Jewish. The apostles, as the foundation stones of the Church and the gospel, had to be Jewish because salvation is of the Jews; the Gentiles were grafted into the promises of God (Rom. 9:4, 5, 11:16-24). So God intended that the foundational apostles be Jews. However, the apostolic qualifications for eldership and deaconship do not require a Jewish heritage for leadership in the local church, but they do restrict women from being elders of the local church (1 Tim. 2:11-15).

47   Cottrell, *Gender Roles & The Bible*, 205.

48   Harper, *Equal and Different*, 38.

49   Clark, *Man and Woman in Christ*, 92.

50   Wayne Grudem, "The Myth of Mutual Submission,' in *CBMW News* 1:4 (October, 1996), 3.

51   Wayne Grudem, "An Open Letter to Egalitarians," in *Journal for Biblical Manhood and Womanhood* 3:1 (March, 1998), 3.

52   Wayne Grudem, "Wives Like Sarah, and Husbands Who Honor Them," in *Recovering Biblical Manhood and Womanhood*, 200.

53   Grudem, "The Myth of Mutual Submission," 3.

54   Grudem, "An Open Letter to Egalitarians," 3.

55   J. Ramsey Michaels, *1 Peter,* Word Biblical Commentary (Waco: Word, 1988), 168.

56   Andrew T. Lincoln, *Ephesians,* Word Biblical Commentary (Dallas: Word, 1990), 367.

57   George W. Knight III, "Husbands and Wives as Analogues of Christ and the Church," in *Recovering Biblical Manhood and Womanhood,* 168.

58   Ibid., 174

59   Nuer, *Man and Woman,* 123

60   Groothuis, *Good News for Women,* 150-158.

61   For a challenge to the meaning *source* for *kephalē* read Wayne Grudem, "The Meaning Source Does Not Exist," in *CBMW News* 3:1 (March, 1998); also "The Meaning of *Kephalē* ('Head'): A Response to Recent Studies," in *Recovering Biblical Manhood & Womanhood,* 425-468; Max Turner, "Modern Linguistics and the New Testament," in *Hearing the New Testament: Strategies for Interpretation,* ed., Joel B. Green (Grand Rapids: Eerdmans, 1995), 165-174.

62   Wayne Grudem, "The Meaning of 'Head' in the Bible: A Simple Question No Egalitarian Can Answer," *CBMWNews* 1:3 (June, 1996), 8.

63   Ibid., 8.

64   Ibid., 8.

65   Grudem, "An Open Letter to Egalitarians," 1, 3.

66   James B. Hurley, *Man and Woman in Biblical Perspective* (Grand Rapids: Zondervan, 1981), 147.

67   D. M. Lloyd-Jones, *Life in the Spirit, in Marriage, Home & Work: An Exposition of Ephesians 5:18 to 6:9* (Grand Rapids: Baker, 1974), 226, 227.

68   William Weinrich, "Man and Woman in Christ," *Lutheran Forum* 29 (May, 1995), 45.

69   John Piper, "A Metaphor of Christ and the Church," *The Standard* (February, 1984), 29.

70   Mary A. Kassian, *Women, Creation and the Fall* (Wheaton: Crossway, 1990), 59.

71   William Hendriksen, *Exposition of Ephesians,* New Testament Commentary (Grand Rapids: Baker, 1967), 250.

72   John MacArthur, Jr., *Ephesians* (Chicago: Moody, 1986), 296.

73   D. M. Lloyd-Jones, *Life in the Spirit, in Marriage, Home & Work,* 213.

74   W. E. Vine, *An Expository Dictionary of New Testament Words, 4* vols. (Kansas City: Walterick, 1969), 3:51.

75   Weinrich, "Man and Woman in Christ," 45.

76   Knight, "Husbands and Wives as Analogues of Christ and the Church," 168.

77   Ernest Best, *Ephesians,* The International Critical Commentary (Edinburgh: T&T Clark, 1998), 559.

78   Walter Bauer, *A Greek-English Lexicon of the New Testament and Other Early Christian Literature,* 2d. ed., trans. William F. Arndt and F. Wilbur Gingrich, rev. F. Wilbur Gingrich and Frederick W. Danker (Chicago: University of Chicago, 1979), s. v. *"anēkō,"* 66. (Hereafter cited as Bauer, A *Greek-English Lexicon of the New Testament.)*

79   Peter T. O'Brien, *Colossians, Philemon,* Word Biblical Commentary (Waco: Word, 1982), 223.

80   Ralph P. Martin, *Colossians: The Church's Lord and The Christian's Liberty* (Grand Rapids: Zondervan, 1972), 130.

81   C. K. Barrett, *The First Epistle to the Corinthians* (New York: Harper, 1968), 156.

82   John Piper and Wayne Grudem, "An Overview of Central Concerns: Questions and Answers," in *Recovering Biblical Manhood and Womanhood*, 88.

83   Robert Lewis and William Hendricks, *Rocking the Roles: Building a Win-Win Marriage* (Colorado Springs: Navpress, 1991), 96, 97.

84   Dorothy Patterson, "The High Calling of Wife and Mother in Biblical Perspective," in *Recovering Biblical Manhood and Womanhood*, 367.

85   Ibid., 373.

86   Kassian, *Women, Creation and the Fall*, 83.

87   Clark, *Man and Woman in Christ*, 630.

88   For the definitive study of 1 Timothy 2:9-15 by eight outstanding evangelical scholars demonstrating the validity of the historic interpretation of this passage read *Women in the Church: A Fresh Analysis of 1 Timothy 2:9-15*, edited by Andreas J. Kostenberger, Thomas R. Schreiner, and H. Scott Baldwin (Grand Rapids: Baker, 1995).

89   Robert and Julia Banks, *The Home Church: Regrouping the People of God for Community and Mission* (Sutherland: Albatross Books, 1986), 82.

90   Thomas R. Schreiner, "An Interpretation of 1 Timothy 2:9-15: A Dialogue with Scholarship," in *Women in the Church*, 120.

91   J. N. D. Kelly, *The Pastoral Epistles: I Timothy, II Timothy, Titus*, Black's New Testament Commentaries (London: Black, 1963), 67.

92   George W. Knight III, *The Pastoral Epistles*, New International Greek Testament Commentary (Grand Rapids: Eerdmans, 1992), 136.

93   John Stott, *Guard the Truth: The Message of I Timothy & Titus* (Downers Grove: InterVarsity, 1996), 84.

94   Clark, *Man and Woman in Christ*, 196, 197.

95   Craig S. Keener, *Paul, Women & Wives: Marriage and Women's Ministry in the Letters of Paul* (Peabody: Hendrickson, 1992), 109.

96   Spencer, *Beyond the Curse*, 88.

97   Henry Scott Baldwin, "A Difficult Word: *authenteō'm* 1 Timothy 2:12," in *Women in the Church*, 65-80.

98   Andreas J. Köstenberger, "A Complex Sentence Structure in 1 Timothy 2:12," in *Women in the Church*, 81-103.

99   It is possible that verse *33b* should be connected to verse 33. If that is correct, the point of women's submission being the universal practice of the church is again made in verses 36-38. However, the context seems to favor verse *33b* as an introduction of the teaching on women's participation in the churches meetings, and not a conclusion to "for God is not a God of confusion but of peace" (v. 33).

100   Gordon D. Fee, *The First Epistle to the Corinthians*, The New International Commentary on the New Testament (Grand Rapids: Eerdmans, 1987), 2.

101   Ibid., 710.

102   Leon Morris, *The First Epistle of Paul to the Corinthians*, The Tyndale New Testament Commentaries (Grand Rapids: Eerdmans, 1958), 202.

103   Ibid., 202.

104   Jack Cottrell, "Christ: a Model for Headship and Submission," in *CBMW News* 2:4 (September, 1997), 8.

105   It is debated whether Paul means husbands and wives or men and women generally. The entire context favors the more general meaning of males and females, men and women, not husbands and wives. Paul speaks of "every man" and "every woman." The major directive concerns men and women praying and prophesying, not family relationships. It is not just husbands who are the image and glory of God, but men generally. It is not exclusively the husband who "has his birth through the woman" but men. In this way 1 Corinthians 11:2-16 is like 1 Timothy 2:8-15 where man and woman generally are the correct renderings.
       The passage would still have application to the husband and wife relationship. If a woman did not have a husband, the headship principle would apply to her father or the local church elders.

106   John 14:28; Phil. 2:6-11; 1 Cor. 11:3, 15:28.

107   S. Lewis Johnson, Jr., "Role Distinctions in the Church: Galatians 3:28," in *Recovering Biblical Manhood and Womanhood,* 164.

108   David Gooding, "Symbols of Headship and of Glory," in *Bible Topics 3* (Belfast: Operation O.F.F.E.R., n.d.), 2.

109   William E. Mouser, Jr., *Five Aspects of Man: A Biblical Theology of Masculinity* (Mountlake Terrace: Wine Press, 1995), 5.6.

110   Barbara K. Mouser, "And the Glory of Man," in *Five Aspects of Woman: A Biblical Theology of Femininity:* A Study Course Offered by the International Council for Gender Studies (Waxahachie, TX: ICGS, 1997), 5.5.

111   Barbara K. Mouser, "Glory of Man," in *Five Aspects of Woman: A Biblical Theology of Femininity,* Course Supplements, 5.4.

112   Barbara K. Mouser, "And the Glory of Man," in *Five Aspects of Woman: A Biblical Theology of Femininity, 5.5.*

113   Harper, *Equal and Different, 22.*

114   James D. G. Dunn, *Romans 9-16,* Word Biblical Commentary (Dallas: Word, 1988), 888.

115   Bauer, *A Greek-English Lexicon of the New Testament,* s.v. *"prostatis,"* 718.

116   James D. G. Dunn, *Romans 9-16,* 895.

117   John Murray, *The Epistle to the Romans,* The New International Commentary on the New Testament (Grand Rapids: Eerdmans, 1968), 231.

118   Brad Blue, "The Influence of Jewish Worship on Luke's Presentation of the Early Church," in *Witness to the Gospel: The Theology of Acts,* eds., I. Howard Marshall and David Peterson (Grand Rapids, Eerdmans, 1998), 481.

119   Stanley J. Grenz with Denise Muir Kjesbo, *Women in the Church: A Biblical Theology of Women in Ministry* (Downers Grove: InterVarsity, 1995), 83.

120   George W. Knight III, *The Pastoral Epistles: A Commentary on the Greek Text,* New International Greek Testament Commentary (Grand Rapids: Eerdmans, 1992), 170-172; Alexander Strauch, *The New Testament Deacon: The Church's Minister of Mercy* (Littleton: Lewis and Roth, 1992), 112-126

121   Cottrell, *Gender Roles & The Bible,* 273.

122   Chris Glaser, *The Word is Out: The Bible Reclaimed for Lesbians and Gay Men* (San Francisco: Harper, 1994), October 3; also Richard Cleaver, *Know My Name: A Gay Liberation Theology* (Louisville: Westminster John Knox, 1995), 27; Michael Vasey, *Strangers and Friends: A New Exploration of Homosexuality and the Bible* (London: Hodder & Stoughton, 1995), 198. The national network of gay and lesbian evangelical Christians is called Evangelicals Concerned.

123   Bruce Waltke, "The Relationship of the Sexes in the Bible," *Crux* 19 (September, 1983), 14.

124   Gordon D. Fee, *Paul's Letter to the Philippians,* The New International Commentary on the New Testament (Grand Rapids: Eerdmans, 1995), 398.

125   Stephen F. Noll of Trinity Episcopal School for Ministry, quoted by David Briggs in "Gay Debate Set on Biblical Battlefield," in the *Rocky Mountain News* (Oct. 27, 1992), 27.

126   Groothuis, *Good News for Women,* 38.

127   D. A. Carson, " 'Silent in the Churches': On the Role of Women in 1 Corinthians 14:33b-36," in *Recovering Biblical Manhood and Womanhood,* 151.

128   John Piper and Wayne Grudem, eds., *Recovering Biblical Manhood and Womanhood: A Response to Evangelical Feminism* (Wheaton: Crossway, 1991); Mary A. Kassian, *Women, Creation and the Fall* (Westchester: Crossway, 1990); Wayne Grudem, "An Open Letter to Egalitarians," in *Journal for Biblical Manhood and Womanhood* 3:1 (March, 1998); Jack Cottrell, *Gender Roles & The Bible: A Critique of Feminist Biblical Interpretation: Gender Roles and the Bible: Creation, the Fall, and Redemption* (Joplin, Mo.: College Press Publishing Company, 1994); Wayne Grudem, "The Meaning *Source* Does Not Exist," *Journal for Biblical Manhood and Womanhood,* 2:5 (Dec. 1997); Andreas J. Kostenberger, Thomas R. Schreiner, and H. Scott Baldwin, eds. *Women in the Church: A Fresh Analysis of 1 Timothy 2:9-15* (Grand Rapids: Baker, 1995); S. M. Baugh, "The Apostle Among the Amazons: A Review Article," *Westminster Theological Journal* 56 (1994): 153-171.

INDEX

Special thanks is due to friends who helped with this book:

Amanda Sorenson, James A. Stahr, David J. MacLeod,
Tom Sorensen, Doyle W. Roth, Barbara Peek,
Allegra James, Paula Graham,
Jonathan Graham, Rachel Bradley

OTHER TITLES FROM
LEWIS & ROTH

**All of these titles can be ordered from
your favorite bookseller or through
Lewis & Roth Publishers
1.800.477.3239 • www.lewisandroth.com**

Oops! I Forgot My Wife offers a fresh and unique approach to encouraging healthy marriages. Communicating biblical truth through humor and story, author Doyle Roth challenges marriages to face their #1 enemy: self-centeredness, equips men for spiritual leadership in the home, provides a helpful resource for counseling and creates a user-friendly approach to evangelism.

Oops! I Forgot My Wife (Paperback; 304 pages)
Oops! Discussion Guide (Paperback; 48 pages)
Oops! Audio CD Set (2 Audio CDs; 158 minutes)

Though a wealth of good material is available on the leadership qualities of courage, charisma, discipline, decisiveness and vision, few books for church leaders include anything about love. *Leading With Love* by Alexander Strauch is written for leaders and teachers at every level of leadership within the local church. Whether you are a Sunday school teacher, youthworker, women's or men's ministry leader, Bible study teacher, small group leader, administrator, music director, elder, deacon, pastor or missionary, love is essential to you and your ministry.

Leading With Love (Paperback; 208 pages)
Leading With Love Study Guide (Paperback; 106 pages)

Hospitality may well be the best means we have to promote close, brotherly love. It is also an effective tool for evangelism. Showing Christ's love to others in a home environment may be the only means Christians have to reach their neighbors for Christ. Ideal for church leaders, *The Hospitality Commands* by Alexander Strauch will also make a difference among the members of your congregation. Study questions and assignments for group discussion are included, making this an excellent resource for small groups and adult Sunday School classes.

The Hospitality Commands (Paperback; 68 pages)